PIPER'S GUIDE TO RESEARCH

PIPER'S GUIDE TO RESEARCH

Jim Piper
Fresno City College

Ray Kytle, Consulting Editor

Dickenson Publishing Company, Inc.
Encino, California, and Belmont, California

Copyright © 1972 by Dickenson Publishing Company, Inc. All rights reserved. No part of this book may be reproduced, stored in a retrieval system, or transcribed, in any form or by any means— electronic, mechanical, photocopying, recording, or otherwise— without the prior written permission of the publisher, 16561 Ventura Boulevard, Encino, California 91316.

Library of Congress Catalog Card Number: 75-189757
Printed in the United States of America
10 9 8 7 6 5 4 3 2 1—76 75 74 73 72

ISBN: 0-8221-00436

TO THE MEMORY OF MY FATHER, INVENTOR

THANKS

- To Mike Snell and Elaine Linden of Dickenson for their invaluable editorial assistance;
- To Ray Kytle of Central Michigan University, my able advisor, who has taught me more about my writing than all the teachers I had in schools —which may prove at least one point this book tries to make;
- To Laurie Harrington, my excellent typist;
- and to the following individuals, publishers, and agencies for graciously allowing me to reprint copyrighted material:

Ballantine Books, Inc.: Excerpt (p. 121) from *The Population Bomb* by Dr. Paul R. Ehrlich. Copyright © 1968 by Paul R. Ehrlich. Reprinted by permission of Ballantine Books, Inc. All rights reserved.

Farrar, Straus & Giroux, Inc.: Excerpt (p. 231) from *The Kandy Kolored Tangerine Flake Streamline Baby* by Tom Wolfe. © 1967 Farrar, Straus & Giroux, Inc. and reprinted with permission.

Harcourt Brace Jovanovich, Inc.: Excerpt (pp. 159, 189, 222) from "A Statement" in *Film Form* by Sergei Eisenstein. Copyright 1949 by Harcourt Brace Jovanovich, Inc. and reprinted by permission.

Houghton Mifflin Company: Excerpt (p. 297) from "Defender of the Faith" in *Goodbye Columbus* by Philip Roth. Copyright 1959 by Philip Roth. Excerpt (p. 311) from *The New Industrial State* by John Kenneth Galbraith. Copyright 1967 by John Kenneth Galbraith. Both reprinted by permission of Houghton Mifflin Company.

International Famous Agency: Excerpt (p. 104) from "The Portable Phonograph" by Walter Van Tilburg Clark. Copyright 1941, 1969 by Walter Van Tilburg Clark. Reprinted by permission of International Famous Agency.

McGraw-Hill Book Company: Excerpt (p. 160) from *Understanding Media* by Marshall McLuhan. Reprinted by permission of the McGraw-Hill Book Company. Copyright 1964 by Marshall McLuhan.

The Macmillan Company: Excerpt (p. 1) from *Democracy and Education* by John Dewey. Copyright 1916 by The Macmillan Company, renewed 1944 by John Dewey. Excerpts (pp. 83, 110, 154, 155, 181, 182, 188, 190) from *The Livliest Art* by Arthur Knight. Copyright 1957 by Arthur Knight. Both reprinted with permission of The Macmillan Company.

The New York Review of Books: Excerpt (p. 101) from "Why We Must Abolish Schooling" by Ivan Illich, *The New York Review of Books,* July 2, 1970, p. 15. Copyright 1970 Ivan Illich. Excerpts (pp. 114, 190, 224, 317) from "Schooling: The Ritual of Progress," *The New York Review of Books,* December 3, 1970, p. 21. Copyright 1970 Ivan Illich. Both reprinted with permission.

Penguin Books Ltd.: Excerpts (pp. 155, 160, 182, 190, 223) from *Film World* by Ivor Montagu. Copyright 1964 by Ivor Montagu. Reprinted by permission of Penguin Books, Inc.

Prentice-Hall, Inc.: Excerpt (pp. 187, 189) from *The American School: A Sociological Analysis* by Patricia Cayo Sexton. Copyright 1967 by Prentice-Hall, Inc. and reprinted with permission.

Random House, Inc.: Excerpts (pp. 87, 90, 191, 306-07) from *The Closed Corporation* by James Ridgeway. © 1968 by James Ridgeway. Reprinted with permission of Random House, Inc.

Saturday Review, Inc.: Excerpts (pp. 119, 190) from "Freedom and Learning: The Need for Choice" by Paul Goodman, May 18, 1968, *Saturday Review.* Copyright 1968 Saturday Review, Inc. Reprinted with permission.

Charles Scribner's Sons: Excerpts (pp. 88, 98-99, 185-86, 188, 209, 308) from *Militarism, U.S.A.* by James A. Donovan. Copyright © 1970 James A. Donovan. Reprinted by permission of Charles Scribner's Sons.

Time, Inc.: Excerpt (p. 308) from "The Military: Servant or Master of Policy?," April 11, 1969. Reprinted by permission from *Time,* The Weekly Newsmagazine; copyright Time, Inc. 1969. Excerpt (p. 292) from "Coed Dorms Put Boys and Girls Together," *Life* Magazine, November 20, 1970, © 1970 Time Inc.

The Washington Monthly: Excerpts (pp. 92, 94, 96, 117, 183, 190, 313) from "Degrees: The Case for Abolition" by David Hapgood, *The Washington Monthly,* August 1969, pp. 6-13. Reprinted by permission of David Hapgood and The Washington Monthly.

The H. W. Wilson Company: Page reproduced (p. 61) from *Readers' Guide to Periodical Literature.* Reprinted by permission of the H. W. Wilson Company.

CONTENTS

III. WRITING

IV. SAMPLES

TO THE INSTRUCTOR

This book has a double mission. First, I hope to give students a research paper guide which is more readable, more useful, and more directly concerned with the spirit of authentic, inductive research than most guides I know of. Second, I hope my readers use this book as a guide to *informed writing* in general, whether such writing takes the form of the traditional library paper, the occasional position paper, or the informal journal based on independent study. This book, then, is based on the simple premise that people write best about what they know best. Overall, my goal is to explain not the research paper, but research, and writing based on research. This distinction, in my opinion, is necessary if we are to make the experience of research worthwhile for our students.

PREFACE: RESEARCH RESURRECTED

Perhaps the reports of the death of worthwhile research in this country have been exaggerated, although it is easy to see how such a rumor could spread. After all, since Hiroshima what passes as responsible scientific research is largely make-work to sustain the military and its various corporate satellites. True, too, since the discovery of Soft Sell too many fine minds have been diverted to market analyses for mass manipulation of tastes and needs, while research into the really urgent problems of the day remains tragically undersubscribed because, apparently, it is neither profitable nor patriotic. And college students also have long sensed that term papers are a drag and that library research is more an exercise in format and correctness than a rewarding adventure in ideas.

But despite these signals of the failing health, or even demise, of worthwhile research in our time, the *spirit* of research lingers and even rallies in odd quarters of society. The lives of many people, especially the young, are filled with experimentation these days, much of it silly, some of it disastrous. But for all the dirty words, cracked heads, tortured frontal lobes, split eardrums, and bitter winters in ragtag communes, something worthwhile occasionally emerges: a new religious insight here, a new mode of self-regulation there, new politics and new living arrangements and, now and then, new definitions of man. Nearly all fruitful pioneer research efforts must first pass through a stage of burned fingers and singed eyebrows.

People seem also to be reading more on their own now. They are perhaps researching with their eyes and minds what others have tried with their hands and bodies. These readers often get burned too, for reading is as dangerous as it is illuminating. They read little-known paperbacks and underground tracts and offbeat newspapers, and they have the potential to push the circulations of specialty magazines like *Ramparts* or *Rolling Stone* high enough to make *Life* and *Reader's Digest* take notice. These magazines in turn respond by becoming somewhat more responsible and daring in their fare. The old heroes, the ballplayers and jet pilots, have been revealed as irrelevant or untrustworthy, and a new type of hero has emerged. He is the folk-rock lyricist, the ecology professor with a pop touch, the writer of mysticism, the pamphleteer, the noon rally speaker; and he deals in words and ideas instead of spitballs and napalm.

Much of this has happened outside the schools, often in spite of the best efforts of the schools to stop it. While the schools were gearing up to help fight the Cold War and assist Proctor & Gamble market yet another unneeded detergent, thousands of Americans were reading on their own about third-world nationalism and the smooth unfreedom of the brand-name society. While the schools were turning out unprofessional engineers and corporation men with little sense of public responsibility, other Americans bothered to inform themselves about what really killed Lake Erie and gooed up the Santa Barbara Channel. While the schools were painting a lyrical, mythical all-white history, a sizeable number of Americans had unveiled a different canvas, more somberly rendered in reds, blacks, and browns.

Now, of course, some schools and colleges have adopted aspects of the underground curriculum. A few colleges may have discovered that their proper mission is to promote individual growth and personal discovery rather than to extrude bodies through a limited number of dies of questionable design. The day of the Summerhill school, the Free U, the experimental college is upon us, and even if these flounder, we should absorb their lesson: Many young people ought to be left alone to read, learn, think, experience, grow, decide, and become according to their own bents.

This book celebrates that goal. But it also insists that the American college, even in its traditional forms, offers much to enhance the clandestine research that goes on all around us in libraries without walls. The American college offers youth many teachers who are learned, mature, and generally humane. It has great libraries and worthy bookstores. It brings people together, young and old, in social-instructive settings where ideas are exchanged. The American college therefore has tremendous resources for making sense of the sometimes muddled conclusions of the underground researchers of our time. Perhaps too it has the will. This book hopes to nourish that will.

PIPER'S GUIDE TO RESEARCH

I
PRELIMINARIES

We sometimes talk as if "original research" were a peculiar prerogative of scientists or at least of advanced students. But all thinking is research, and all research is native, original, with him who carries it on, even if everybody else in the world already is sure of what he is looking for.

—*John Dewey*

1
The Research Paper and You

Colleges are changing all the time, usually for the better. Several hundred years ago only young men went to college, and all their classes were conducted in Latin or Greek. And it wasn't until relatively recently that students were allowed to select among a wide range of courses and majors. When colleges do change, they usually respond to certain broader social changes brought on by scientific discoveries, economic depressions, and wars—especially wars. No one knows for sure how our colleges will change during the seventies and beyond, but this book is betting on one sure, lasting change for the better: Students will be allowed to explore alternatives to the classroom for learning what they want to learn.

Which brings us to the subject of this book: the library research paper. If approached in a positive, useful way, the research paper gives you the chance to read, think, and write on your own about matters *you* feel are important. You may not be allowed to set up your own courses, choose your own textbooks, and write your own tests—nor may you want to—but when you write a research paper in college you are free to explore virtually any topic and come to a variety of conclusions. The research paper, in short, provides the freedom to learn that many students today, perhaps yourself, seem to want.

The research papers you write in college could take up where your courses and textbooks leave off. If, for instance, an engineering student feels his course work is not answering such questions as the responsibilities of engineers in cleaning up the environment or the limits of technology in solving some of our complex problems, he might elect to follow up one of these matters in a research project leading to a paper. Or a student in a psychology class might wonder what feelings of insecurity and strong belief in God have to do with each other. If his teacher can't help him, the student might explore this question through outside reading, and later write a paper about what he has learned. Another student who wants to make movies the way a poet makes poems may be disappointed that none of his classes will give him a chance to study film as art. Perhaps this student will look into some aspect of the art of film as a topic for a research paper.

If some research projects are hatched because college courses don't always answer students' questions, other research projects are born because courses raise certain questions students find interesting. This is especially true of introductory or survey courses that move so fast they can't explore details and sidelights in depth. Suppose a student in a history class learns that the ideas of Karl Marx had some influence on the organized labor movement in America. If the student finds this information interesting, or even threatening, he might want to read on his own about Marxism and labor unions to get the connection between the two straight.

When you write a research paper you become a sort of expert, and you may have more respect for other people who have special knowledge about issues. You may be more inclined to look into these issues yourself. And just as important, when you undertake a research project you learn to work mainly on your own, pacing yourself and setting your own goals.

What is a research paper?

A research paper is something like a scrapbook. Most scrapbooks are assembled around a single subject, such as space exploration or horse shows or sports cars or the career of a certain public figure or the fortunes of a pro football team or the progress of a love affair. Into the scrapbook goes a variety of odds and ends—snapshots, newspaper and magazine clippings, autographs, letters, locks of hair, pressed flowers, torn admission tickets, and other pasteable memorabilia. Most scrapbooks have a sort of order and method about them; the material is arranged usually in order of time with the oldest and most faded material pasted in first and the most recent last. The scrapbook often says something, too, at least indirectly. It says, "Space travel is exciting," or, "Paul Newman has become more serious over the years," or, "It's the little things that are so important to John and me." Finally, many scrapbooks feature a sort of running commentary inked in between the photos and clippings to explain what all the stuff means: "This was the best horse show all year," or, "I nearly died when we lost this game," or, "John fell into the lake after this picture was taken and all his M&M's melted."

The research paper borrows much from the spirit of the scrapbook. It too is assembled around a central subject. It also brings together an assortment of odds and ends, namely, facts, statistics, expert opinion, and case studies. Like a scrapbook, the research paper has a certain order to it, and like many scrapbooks it includes a running commentary to tie in all the facts, quotations, and so on.

But the writer of a research paper doesn't merely fatten out his paper the way the keeper of a scrapbook accumulates clippings and photos between covers. The writer of a research paper is more definite about his purpose. He wants to make a point in his paper, a central idea that clearly ties together all the material he presents. He hits on this central idea after a period of outside reading. He gets his idea across to his reader by reconstructing what he has learned from his readings. He pieces together the most pertinent information and expert opinion so that the reader will arrive at the same conclusions he did. Much of what is written by the researcher, his running commentary, is meant only to provide transitions between separate pieces of information or to comment on the significance of the information. It is this combination of information and running commentary that gets the idea across to the reader.

College research papers can be almost any length. Some are just a few pages long. Most, however, are at least five to ten pages in length, and a few run to twenty pages or more. The length of the paper or papers you write with this book will probably depend on how your teacher decides to use the book and how it relates to other reading and writing assignments he makes. The book stresses the longer paper, but it also gives suggestions for writing shorter, less ambitious papers, as well as for keeping journals and participating in group discussions based on independent study.

Originality

The completed research paper, like any scrapbook, is a unique creation, something that borrows from many books and magazines, but something that is different, too, from any single book or part of a book or magazine article. The whole point of research is to discover something new by assembling in a unique way what is already known. This is the art of research. Like any form of art, research joins separate details to produce a meaningful total effect. Consider, for example, these pieces of information:

1. An increasing number of employers are now requiring BA degrees of their applicants.
2. Studies show that employees with BA degrees do not produce more or work better than employees on the same job who do not have BA degrees.

Considered separately, these findings have their own implications. The first implies, among other things, that employers value the BA degree. The second implies that college training has little to do with job proficiency. But the two pieces of information together imply something else again: Employers may require the BA degree for reasons other than obtaining good workers. In much the same way, poets combine words, musicians sounds, and filmmakers images to produce works of art.

Because no two people combine details in the same way or see identical meanings in them, your research paper will be an original effort. It will be unlike anything else in the world, and that is certainly something to be proud of. It could happen, however, that your conclusions may be similar to conclusions other people have already arrived at. But this doesn't mean your paper is not original —for you. Originality, as that term is used in this book, means you have done some outside reading, and have thought about what you have read, and have finally come to conclusions that are *new to you.* You could *not* have come to these conclusions without informing yourself and reflecting upon what you have learned. If you have been serious about using the opportunity for research to find ideas new to you, the chances are very good that these ideas will be new to other people as well. But even if ideas you think are new strike other people as rather commonplace, *you* are the important point of reference. It is you for whom research has yielded new ideas.

An overview of your research project

Another way to describe a research paper is to explain what you should do to write one. The paper itself is the end of a sort of journey, from uncertainty to certainty, and like all journeys, your research project will be more direct and enjoyable if planned as a series of "legs" or steps. Each step described below corresponds to a separate chapter in Parts II and III of this book. Each of these chapters concludes with a brief, specific assignment to help you complete the step the chapter takes up.

Step 1: Formulating the research question. A good way to make sure your journey takes a more or less direct route is to base your research on a question you want to answer through reading and writing. Chapter 3 suggests a number of topics on which research questions may be based. Without a specific question, your investigations could lead you into so many aspects of your topic you could have trouble making sense of what you read. With a question, you will know what to read and what not to read; you will also know when to stop reading.

Step 2: Locating materials to read. Chapter 4 is meant to help you find whatever materials you need to read to answer your research question. It explains how to get around in the library, and it suggests other places in your community you might visit to gather useful reading material.

Step 3: Reading and note-taking. Now that you have your hands on some materials, you will need to read and take notes about whatever pertains to your research question. Chapter 5 offers suggestions on how to read, what to look for, and how to take notes.

Step 4: Posing the thesis and refining it. Next, you pose an answer to your research question, a set of conclusions that grew out of your readings. Then you combine these conclusions into what is called a *thesis.* The thesis is very important because it will guide the writing of your paper. You want to be sure it says what you mean and will be clear to people who later read your paper. You may need, therefore, to revise or refine your thesis, and this could mean additional follow-up readings. Chapter 6 takes up these matters.

Step 5: Outlining the paper. Before you can write your paper, you need to organize your thoughts. An outline often helps. Chapter 7 shows you how to develop a working outline from your notes and your thesis.

Step 6: Writing the paper. Writing your paper means, in general, stating your thesis and then reconstructing your reading and note-taking in support of your thesis. Chapter 8 explains the transformation of the outline into a paper.

Step 7: Finishing the paper. Finally, you should put your finished paper into a format the reader can follow. Chapter 9 explains the format or appearance of the finished paper.

Part IV presents sample papers, long and short, for you to examine. Many chapters in Parts II and III include examples, ideas, and notes that were used to produce two longer papers found in Chapter 10. Thus if you read this book from beginning to end you will trace the birth, growth, and completion of two research projects. Part IV also explains how research might lead to journals and discussion groups—two worthwhile alternatives to formal papers.

AFTERCHAPTER

Activities

1. Discuss in class: If courses in high school or college don't always answer students' personal questions, whose fault is this: The courses', for not pointing out specific applications? The students', for failing to relate to general ideas?

2. Make a list of questions you feel your courses in high school or college should have taken up and answered, but did not.

3. Make a list of interesting points your courses in high school or college raised but did not pursue. Phrase these points as questions: What else would you like to know about them?

4. Select one question you wrote for 2 or 3 above and write a short paper about it. You might

a) try to answer the question based on your experience and present knowledge,

OR

b) elaborate on either the question or the class it pertains to,

OR

c) discuss the question with other students with similar questions, and base your paper on the ideas that grew out of the discussion.

2
Strategies of Inquiry

Before deciding *what* to research, you might give some thought to *how* to research, how to pattern all the thinking, reading, and writing you'll invest in your research project. This chapter takes up eight common patterns or strategies of inquiry. One or two of these strategies could point the way for you. They could suggest a research question. Often they imply what kinds of material you should read and what kinds of information you should be alert for. These strategies may also help you shape your conclusions and organize the findings of your paper. These eight strategies are:

1. *Itemization:* Listing several important aspects of a topic.
2. *Classification:* Grouping several aspects of a topic into a small number of all-inclusive classifications.
3. *Comparison:* Determining the similarities and/or differences between two topics.
4. *Cause and effect:* Determining the cause or causes of a certain event or development or the effects of an event or development.
5. *Problem and solution:* Advancing a solution for a certain problem.
6. *Time.* Tracing something that has changed, or has remained stable, over a period of time.
7. *Deduction.* Applying general principles to specific topics or issues.
8. *Relation.* Establishing the connection between at least two topics or two aspects of one topic.

There are, of course, many other ways to pattern research; your teacher might add to this list, just as these strategies are often combined effectively. But these eight common strategies should suggest, at least, that research does have order, purpose, and direction.

Now for a closer look at these strategies.

To itemize means to make a list. Many research projects entail a listing of key points or aspects of a topic. The finished paper may not include all points uncovered during research, but it will take up those the researcher feels are most important. Example:

Research question: What steps can consumers take to fight pollution?

Conclusions based on readings: Consumers can
1) boycott products that contribute to pollution;
2) buy only products that can be reused or recycled;
3) mount campaigns to encourage industry and government to fight pollution;
4) try to reduce personal waste and litter;
5) teach their children to be thoughtful consumers;
6) teach their children respect for the environment.

Thesis: There is much that consumers can do to minimize pollution.

In this example, the research question implies that the researcher would have to read to make a list, or to itemize, the courses of action open to consumers who want to fight pollution. Each of the conclusions, or courses of action, is based on reading and note-taking. The thesis is a summary of all conclusions, as well as the central idea that will guide the writing of the paper. The paper, we can expect, will enlarge on the six courses of action consumers can take.

At first glance, classification, as a strategy of inquiry, seems identical to itemization, but there are important differences. The person who classifies considers a lot of different aspects of a topic and groups them under a small number of major headings. The major headings are meant to be all-inclusive: Any aspect of the topic should fall under one of the headings. Itemization is open-ended; only the most important aspects of a topic are listed. Classification attempts to enclose the topic. In the following example, the research question about consumers fighting pollution has been altered slightly to anticipate a classification, rather than an itemization, of courses of action.

Research question: What types of action can consumers take to fight pollution?

Conclusions based on readings:
1. Economic action
    A. Boycott products that contribute to pollution.
    B. Buy only products that can be reused or recycled.
2. Political action
    A. Mount campaigns to encourage industry and gov-
       ernment to fight pollution.
3. Personal action
    A. Try to reduce personal waste and litter.
    B. Teach children to be thoughtful consumers.
    C. Teach children respect for the environment.

Thesis: There are three major ways consumers can help
fight pollution: through economic, political, and personal
action.

Thus a paper based on this thesis would be structured in three
parts, each developing, by itemizing, major courses of action. But
note how "A. Mount campaigns to encourage industry and government to fight pollution" stands alone under the heading "2. Political
action." Perhaps there are other types of political action consumers
can take, just as more than one type of action was listed under the
other headings. Additional readings might reveal that consumers
can also
    B. Support only political candidates with records for
       fighting pollution.

But to itemize is not always to classify. Often it is sufficient merely
to list a few important points or aspects and leave it at that. Classification sometimes comes off labored and high-blown if used when
it isn't needed. But if a list of aspects grows too long—say, ten
reasons for dropping college—classification helps to group the aspects and make relationships clearer—two main reasons for dropping college: voluntary and involuntary.

Comparison

Some research projects deal in two topics rather than one. The
two topics have something to do with each other, and the researcher wants to investigate the similarities or the differences between them. Sometimes he wants to read about both similarities
and differences, but the thesis that emerges from research will
usually stress one or the other.

Research question: How do the goals of women's rights
groups compare with the goals of older civil rights groups?
Conclusions based on readings:
1. Both women and ethnic minorities are working to end
   discrimination in employment.

2. Both want their members to be recognized as individuals, rather than "type cast" as members of groups.
3. Both seek economic independence from other groups —women from men, blacks from whites.
4. Minority groups have been more successful in winning widespread support for their cause than women have.

Thesis: Both women's rights groups and older civil rights movements are primarily concerned with the issue of dignity.

Evidently, the paper written from this thesis will stress similarities rather than differences, and the key phrase "the issue of dignity" is the researcher's way of unifying his conclusions. The fourth conclusion, about the differing success of the two movements, will apparently be deemphasized in the paper, or not mentioned at all.

Comparisons are perhaps most useful for exploring similarities between two topics that are not generally regarded to be similar, or for discovering differences between topics most people feel are nearly alike. Everyone knows, for instance, that the black civil rights movement and the more recent Mexican-American civil rights movement of the Southwest have obvious similarities, but inquiry meant to discover differences between the two movements might help the researcher understand both movements better. Everyone knows that poetry and advertising are quite different forms of communication, but they may also have important similarities worth investigating. Research aimed at comparing two topics requires that the researcher read about both topics and itemize important similarities or differences.

Cause and effect

Research projects intended to explore causes and effects usually begin with rather well-known events or developments and proceed to less well-known matters. Either the cause or the effect may be well known. The object is to explore the link in the cause-effect chain that is less well known, open to speculation. Example:

Research question: What impact did the advent of sound in 1927 have on the later development of film art?

Conclusions based on readings:

1. D. W. Griffith and Sergei Eisenstein pioneered the art of film editing during the silent film era.
2. The optical sound track was introduced by businessmen in 1927 to increase movie attendance.
3. The earliest sound films used sound clumsily and excessively.

4. At first sound threatened to cancel the achievements of filmmakers such as Griffith and Eisenstein because it distracted from the visual factor.
5. Filmmakers of the thirties learned to use sound to extend the editing principles of the silent era: Not only picture-to-picture, but sound-to-picture and sound-to-sound relationships were explored.

Thesis: The advent of sound in 1927 at first posed a threat to the developing art of cinema and only gradually won a place in the repertoire of editing principles established during the silent era.[1]

In this example, conclusions 2 and 3 represent readings about the cause (the advent of sound). Conclusions 4 and 5 deal with effects, short term and long term. A paper based on this thesis would, of course, stress effects, since these are less well known than the cause.

Other research projects patterned to explore causes and effects might focus more on causes than on effects, if causes are less well known. For example, everyone has heard about a so-called gap between the generations, but few people have systematically explored the reasons or causes for the gap, and those who have don't often agree. Inquiry into this topic would focus primarily on the causes of the generation gap. Some warnings: The researcher who explores causes of well-known events or developments must guard against simplistic or faulty conclusions. Rarely can complex developments, such as the generation gap, be attributed to a single cause. Permissive child-raising may have contributed to the rebelliousness of some youth, but it probably isn't the only cause. Often several possible causes need to be itemized and compared, and conclusions drawn about the relative importance of each—an example of mixing strategies of inquiry.

Also, it is possible to confuse cause and effect. Are permissive child-raising practices a cause of the generation gap, or are both really effects of deeper causes, such as rapid cultural changes that sweep away older ideas? Finally, two things that seem to vary together may have no cause-effect connection at all. It is true that for a while the Dow-Jones stock market increased as students became more rebellious, but it is not likely that one development had much to do with the other. If you intend to connect two events or trends causally, you have to be sure that one brought on the other.

---

[1]See Chapter 10 for a completed paper based on this thesis.

This strategy leads the researcher first to read about a particular problem, then to consider possible solutions. Again, the solutions may have to be itemized, compared, and weighed. And like inquiry into causes, the investigation of solutions requires good judgment. The researcher should not be overly impressed by simple solutions to complicated problems. He should also decide whether he intends to focus his research on the effects of the problem, the causes, or both:

Research question: What should be done to reduce over-population in underdeveloped countries?

Conclusions based on readings:

1. Underdeveloped countries often cannot produce enough food to feed their rapidly growing populations.
2. Abortions do not get at the causes of overpopulation.
3. The newer contraceptive devices, however effective, are often resisted because of local customs and religious practices.
4. In more advanced and better educated societies, families voluntarily limit their sizes.
5. The basic solution to overpopulation in underdeveloped countries is to eliminate ignorance and upgrade standards of living.

Thesis: Abortion and contraceptive devices are less effective measures for reducing the populations of underdeveloped countries than long-range social and economic measures.

A paper about this thesis would first explain the problem (conclusion 1), then consider various solutions (conclusions 2, 3, and 4), and finally recommend one best solution (conclusion 5).

The researcher who traces something over a period of time is interested in change or lack of change. He may draw a comparison with something else that has changed, or he may read about causes, effects, problems, or solutions. But his main job is to discover change or stability over a period of time. It is enough to discover *that* something has changed, but one is not obliged to read about *why* something has changed or whether the change is desirable or not —unless one wants to. Example:

Research question: How have methods of waging war changed from Korea to Vietnam?

Conclusions based on readings:
1. In Korea the opposing armies formed well-defined battle lines, or a front.
2. The political views of civilians had little effect on the outcome of the Korean war.
3. In the early years of the Vietnam war, allied forces tried to form a front and ignored the political views of civilians.
4. The Viet Cong, however, rather than forming a front, employed hit-and-run guerrilla tactics and actively sought to change the political views of the civilians in areas they controlled.
5. Later on, allied forces also sought the political support of civilians and developed counterguerrilla tactics.

Thesis: Conventional methods of waging war were modified in Vietnam to stress guerilla tactics and the political indoctrination of civilians.

Conclusion 4 suggests the cause for the change in war tactics noted in conclusion 5. The conclusions also imply a comparison— between tactics in Korea and tactics in Vietnam. But the thesis stresses the nature of the change rather than causes or comparisons, and so would the finished paper.

Deduction

The researcher who proceeds deductively explores certain general principles or broad ideas that can be applied to his specific research topic. The research topic is placed in a larger frame of reference that makes the topic better understood. Example:

Research question: Does the government have the right to hasten school integration by bussing students?

Conclusions based on readings:
1. The government has the right to take any measure that will benefit the entire nation.
2. Integration of schools is in the best interests of the entire nation.
3. Schools usually draw students from local neighborhoods.
4. Many neighborhoods are not yet fully integrated.
5. Bussing therefore is the only way to achieve integration.

Thesis: Court-ordered bussing can be justified as being in the best interests of the nation.

A paper based on this thesis would first present the general principles advanced by conclusions 1 and 2. Then it would present certain facts gathered in conclusions 3 and 4. Finally, it would apply all these principles and facts to the topic of bussing. In effect, the writer of the paper is saying that the issue of bussing is understandable only when related to certain relevant general principles and to facts pertaining to the general principles.

Deduction often has a three-part structure: a first or major premise, a second or minor premise, and a conclusion. Example:

> *First premise:* The government has no right to force changes unacceptable to the majority of people.
>
> *Second premise:* Bussing of students to achieve integration is opposed by the majority of people.
>
> *Conclusion:* The government has no right to push bussing.

Another example:

> *First premise:* The government has a duty to protect the interests of minorities.
>
> *Second premise:* Bussing is in the interests of minorities.
>
> *Conclusion:* The government has a duty to promote bussing.

The premises of a deductive strategy should be arguable or reasonable, and the conclusion should follow naturally and logically. The goal is to assemble enough information and expert commentary to justify the premises. If the premises are reasonable, and if the second premise can be shown to relate to the first premise, the conclusion also should be reasonable.

Relation

Often research projects begin in a hunch that two topics or two aspects of a topic are connected in some way. The whole object of research is to discover the connection. The connection could lead the reader into one or more of these strategies of research:

1. Comparison. Perhaps the two topics have common elements that are worth learning about: The relationship between poetry and advertising is that both render reality through symbols.

2. Cause and Effect. It may be discovered that the two topics have a cause-effect connection: The relationship between war and inflation is that the cost of war heats up the economy and drives up prices. Or the two topics may be affected by a third factor: The relationship between a rising crime rate and growing welfare rolls is that both are functions of basic social and economic problems.

3. Deduction. Both topics may be associated with important general principles: The relationship between library research and laboratory research is that both should be pursued in a spirit of open-mindedness.

Here is an example that combines all three ways topics may be related:

Research question: What is the connection between the so-called military-industrial complex and our system of college education?

Conclusions based on readings:

1. Large institutions often become very inefficient and self-serving.
2. The expansionist military-industrial complex led us into Vietnam at a great cost of lives, money, and resources.
3. Many of our leading universities are deeply involved in war-related research—often at the expense of students.
4. Colleges, too, have been growing, and education as a whole is America's second biggest industry after Defense.
5. Studies show a poor relationship between performance in college and later performance on the job.
6. If the colleges were scaled down, viable alternatives for learning might flourish.

Thesis: Like other overgrown institutions, our college system has become self-serving and wasteful, and its influence should now be restricted to allow alternatives to flourish.[2]

Thus the paper would relate the twin topics of the military and the colleges by (a) comparison (both have become big business), (b) cause and effect (the war pulled many universities into the orbit of the military-industrial complex), and (c) deduction (most large institutions tend to be inefficient and self-serving, a principle that can apply to both the military and the colleges).

Mixing strategies

These eight strategies can be mixed effectively, as the last example about the military and the colleges shows. Cause and effect and problem and solution often go together: certain effects produce problems in need of solutions. Causes and solutions often are compared. Explanations of causes or solutions may require a deductive strategy or a relating of specific matters to general principles. Itemization, as we have seen, is used in nearly all research projects, and will occasionally lead to classification—of causes, effects, problems, solutions, and so forth.

Mixing strategies in these ways can produce hybrid forms which, like many hybrids, are stronger and better than their purer ances-

---

[2]See Chapter 10 for a completed paper based on this thesis.

tors. Mixing strategies also multiplies the possibilities of thought nearly endlessly. The success of your research project could turn on your finding the most appropriate strategy or strategies for directing your reading, thinking, and writing.

AFTERCHAPTER

Activities

1. Which of the following examples of deductive thinking strike you as having (a) untenable premises, (b) questionable conclusions, or (c) basically sound premises and conclusions. Explain your choices.

   A. Poetry is the right words in the right order. Good advertising copy is the right words in the right order. Good advertising copy is poetry.

   B. It is murder to take the life of any being with a soul. A human embryo has a soul. Abortion is murder.

   C. Murder is the unlawful killing of another person with malice aforethought. Abortion is not performed with malice aforethought. Abortion is not murder.

   D. Anyone who criticizes his country is unpatriotic. Many American youths have voiced criticism of their government's foreign policy. The youth of America are unpatriotic.

   E. A traitor is one who takes action against his country for personal gain. Many American youths have taken action against their country, but they have not sought personal gain. These youths are not traitors, though they may be guilty of other offenses.

   F. Every person has a right to develop his or her full potential. Women who must raise children are denied the right to develop to their full potential. The government should establish free childcare centers for women who want to work.

   G. The government has no right to pass laws infringing on the private lives of citizens. Smoking marijuana is a private activity. The government has no right to pass laws prohibiting the smoking of marijuana.

   H. All communist countries have government-run dental programs. Senators Blatz and Blump have advocated government-run dental programs. Senators Blatz and Blump are communists.

2. Explain how the pairs of topics below might be related by either (a) comparison, or (b) cause and effect, or (c) deduction. Might some pairs of topics be related in more than one way? If the topics are related by cause and effect, does one cause the other, or are both affected by third factors?

   A. Air pollution and water pollution.
   B. Sex and the automobile.
   C. Premarital sex and divorce.
   D. Pioneers and hippie communes.
   E. Violence in the media and violence in society.
   F. Science and religion.
   G. Any two courses you are taking.

3. Select any five topics from the list below. Match each topic with an appropriate strategy for writing a thesis sentence. Mix strategies if you wish. Write thesis sentences for all five topics. Base your thesis sentences on your opinions, experience, or present knowledge.

A. Sex education
B. Cigaret smoking
C. Pornography
D. The death of God
E. Pets
F. The ideal society
G. Your city
H. A hobby
I. TV programming
J. Dating
K. Crime
L. Parents and teenagers
M. Going to college
N. Survival
O. A topic of your choice

Examples:
1) *Topic:* Pets
   Strategy: Classification
   Thesis: Pets may be divided into two classes, those requiring a lot of attention and those requiring little attention.
2) *Topic:* Los Angeles's traffic problem
   Strategy: Problem and solution
   Thesis: Mass rapid transit is the only way to solve the traffic problem of Los Angeles.

4. Select any thesis you wrote for activity 5. Write a four- or five-paragraph essay based on the thesis. Let the first paragraph serve as an introduction leading up to the thesis. Let the last paragraph serve as a conclusion. In the two or three paragraphs following the introduction, flesh out the ideas of your thesis: Explain terms, give examples, develop your ideas by following the strategy suggested by your thesis.

Below is a sample essay utilizing the strategies of comparison and cause and effect:

COMPETITION AND VIOLENCE

Nearly everyone wants to know why there is so much violence in our society, why so much killing and mugging and child beating and terror bombing. A number of explanations have been offered, such as permissive child-raising practices, a breakdown of traditional values, certain social or economic inequalities. Anthropologists, however, may have uncovered a more fundamental cause of violence: the competitive ethic that pervades our society. According to anthropologist Geoffrey Gorer, human societies that deemphasize the competitive life are much less prone to violence than our society seems to be.

The African Pygmy society is small and simple, but the cooperative ethic is strong. Individuals work together to gather food, produce tools, and erect huts. Rather than warring with other tribes or passing their time in competitive games, Pygmies prefer sensuous or relaxing activities such as eating, drinking, dancing, and conversation. Men do not have to "prove" themselves by feats of strength and courage. And anthropologists have noted that fighting, murder, theft, and rape are virtually unknown among the Pygmies.

We Americans, on the other hand, are encouraged to compete and prove ourselves nearly as soon as we can walk and talk. The home, the school, the neighborhood, the job—all these are settings for a sort of combat, and the "winners" among us rise to the top at the expense of the "losers." Our society teaches rivalry, domination, even hatred. When we are actually encouraged to commit psychological violence, physical violence may come easier to us.

It is, of course, a long way from competing for grades to commiting murder. And any particular act of violence can certainly be traced to many causes. But it may be possible that many apparently senseless acts of violence are connected in some way to the highly competitive nature of our society.

II
RESEARCH

What does education often do? It makes a straight-cut ditch out of a free, meandering brook.

—*H. D. Thoreau*

I have never let my schooling interfere with my education.

—*Mark Twain*

3

Formulating a Research Question

Someone once responded to the well-known advice, "Christ is the answer," by asking, "What was the question?" This person was, in his own way, stressing first things first—questions before answers. Other people have noted that if we ask silly questions, we get silly answers. Unless we are clear on what we want to know, we won't know what to look for, or what it means if we blunder across it.

Good questions are no less important for research projects. They lend purpose to reading, thinking, and writing. They suggest what to look for and when to stop looking. The student who researches without a specific question may find himself looking into so many areas and aspects of a topic that his conclusions probably won't relate well and his paper will likely turn out badly organized. A research question limits inquiry so conclusions can be more sensibly related and the paper more easily written.

Topics for research questions

Some students feel they aren't especially interested in topics they have to look up in libraries. They may select a topic to research they are only lukewarm about just to get the assignment done and handed in on time. Often, however, these students have dismissed as too commonplace or personal topics that do indeed have potential for worthwhile research. What follows is a survey of topics which are probably of concern to nearly everyone. Chances are that several will appeal to you.

Each topic is accompanied by a number of sample research questions. The questions have been worded to suggest at least one of the strategies of inquiry we examined in the last chapter. If you don't find a question to research after reading this chapter, at least you'll have an idea of the kinds of topics and strategies that can be pursued.

Work and career The kind of work a person does helps define that person, for himself and for other people. Anyone undecided about his choice of work (or choice of major in college) naturally feels incomplete and untried. You may want to use the opportunity for research to look into jobs and professions that interest you, but perhaps scare you a little, too. If you are a young woman, you may face an even greater question—to work or not to work, to pursue a career or be a housewife. Male or female, you might benefit from reading to answer one of the following questions pertaining to jobs and careers:

Itemization. What are the advantages and disadvantages of a certain profession or career? What are the working conditions, the responsibilities, the opportunities for advancement and personal satisfaction?

Classification. What are the different types of jobs available to persons with certain special interests (a love of animals or aviation) or special abilities (handicrafts or athletics)? What types of jobs are available to college students who major in subjects not directly job-related, such as English, biology, or ethnic studies? What types of jobs are available to junior college students who do not transfer to four-year colleges? What types of jobs are open to four-year college students who drop out before graduation?

Time. What is the history of a certain profession or job? Have benefits and working conditions become better or worse? What about the future of a certain job? Will opportunities and salaries improve?

Comparison. What are the differences and similarities between related jobs (vocational nurse and registered nurse, technician and engineer)? How do job opportunities for men and women compare? How do job opportunities for whites and nonwhites compare?

Problem and solution. How can work (or a certain job) be made more personally satisfying? What problems has automation caused, and how can they be met? What problems of employment do certain groups of people face (the young, the old, the nonwhite, the handicapped, the returning veteran)?

Politics Becoming politically aware means more than just voting or joining a political party. It means achieving a consistency of thought and action derived from deep convictions about how society should be structured. When you become aware of the reasons for your political decisions, you understand how you relate to society as a whole and to the government that contributes, or fails to contribute, to the betterment of that society. You vote for candidates whose ideas about society coincide with yours. You demand that candidates take stands on specific issues and legislative measures. You understand how manner, appearance, and promotional campaigns are usually less important than a candidate's integrity and qualifications.

Classification. How might political views be classified? How might liberal views be classified? How might conservative views be classified?

Comparison. How do the political views of two groups differ (the young and the old, the rich and the poor, whites and non-whites)? How do the political views of two prominent candidates or two public figures differ?

Problem and solution. What laws or programs need to be enacted to meet a particular problem in society? What special interest groups oppose these laws or programs? What groups support them? How can the activities of Congress be streamlined or speeded up? What can be done to make government (or one agency or service) more responsible to people?

Deduction. Under what conditions, if any, may a person commit civil disobedience for political reasons? Where do the prerogatives of government end and the rights of citizens begin? How might these prerogatives and rights be applied to specific issues (the draft, protest, taxes, drug laws, medical care, education)? On what constitutional basis have the courts handed down decisions of social or political consequence (the draft, education, conspiracy, crime)?

Relation. How do political views relate to income, social class, personality, occupation, race, or ethnic origin? What is the connection between politics and pollution, war, crime, education, or urban renewal?

Religion If some people vote for or against political candidates for questionable reasons—pretty wives, snappy TV commercials, good looks—other people go to church for reasons just as silly—to meet dates, to show off new clothes, to keep parents happy. Perhaps one's religious life ought to spring from deep convictions about the nature of God, man, and the afterlife. If you have ever had questions about sin, salvation, the correct form of worship, or your relationship to God, you might want to explore an aspect of religion for your research project.

Itemization. What are the tenets or beliefs of a certain denomination or religion?

Comparison. How are any two religions or denominations similar or different? How do the religious views of young people differ, if at all, from those of their elders? How do hippies' religious views differ from those of other people?

Cause and effect. Does the use of drugs bring about religious experiences? What makes people seek out exotic fringe religions and cults? Why are traditional religious beliefs and practices under attack today? Why are priests and nuns leaving the Catholic Church, and what long-term effect will this have on the Church? What will be the consequences for either individuals or society if traditional religious beliefs and practices are swept away? What does religion do for the individual?

Relation. Does science threaten religious values or confirm them? Should churches take stands on such issues as birth control, abortion, capital punishment, crime, war, and civil rights? Should businesses run by churches be tax exempt? How do religious preferences relate to such matters as politics, age, life style, occupation or personality? How does religion (or a certain denomination) relate to other systems of thought, such as existentialism, Marxism, psychoanalysis, mysticism, and Zen Buddhism?

Problems of a personal nature Students occasionally select topics to research of a rather personal nature. This doesn't mean their research papers become windows thrown open on their private lives. It is possible to research and write about personal problems in an impersonal and objective way. No one knows these students are really writing about themselves. For example, a stutterer is usually a little reluctant to talk about his problem. But a stutterer who researches, say, the causes or cures of stuttering can write about stuttering generally, not personally, and no one need know his research problem is really his way to work out a personal problem. Teachers are professionals, and like doctors, lawyers, and priests, they are compelled to reveal nothing about their clients' private lives. Teachers are also human beings, and they are usually willing to help students find ways to research problems of a personal nature with dignity.

Other examples of personal problems: sexual relations, dating, abortion, the use of drugs, draft evasion, trouble with the law, personality problems, divorce, family problems, long-term illness, physical disability, and confusion about goals or life style. All of these problems can be researched objectively. Not all of them can be worked out by research alone, but who knows where the research could lead? Some strategies for formulating research questions dealing with personal problems:

Cause and effect. What brought on the so-called sexual revolution? Where will it lead? What are the long-term effects of using a certain drug? What causes divorce? How does divorce affect younger children?

Problem and solution. How can people overcome shyness? How can the physically handicapped, such as cripples, lead normal, productive lives? What help is available to people with emotional disorders?

Classification. What are the alternatives to military service? What drugs produce what effects?

Comparison. How do hippies differ from other people? How do political radicals differ from moderates? What are the advantages and disadvantages of certain contraceptive devices? How does a conscientious objector differ from a draft dodger?

Relation. How are child-raising habits related to the later personality of children? How are sexual or dating problems related to such matters as drug use, home life, personality, and social class background?

Hobbies and special interests What are your interests? Popular music? Cars? Fashions? Horses? Hiking? Flying? Stamp collecting? Ham radio? Photography? Politics? Sports? Poetry? Painting? Filmmaking? Astrology? You might use the opportunity for research to extend your knowledge about a hobby or special interest. For instance, the student who is an amateur photographer might look into how photography, as an art form, compares with painting or sculpture as an art form. Or he might survey critical commentary about the works of several famous photographers and then form general principles about the nature of great photography. In short, you should adopt a slightly more intellectual attitude toward your special interest so your paper doesn't end up merely a rundown of how-tos and dos and don'ts. Some suggestions:

Classification. What are the various trends and styles of popular music today? What kinds of horses are best for different purposes —riding, racing, breeding, and so forth? What sports or types of sports promote physical fitness best?

Comparison. Which type of racing car is better, piston or turbine? How does filmmaking compare with other arts, such as painting and poetry? How does camping in the mountains compare with camping in the desert?

Time. Where did our popular music come from? Where is it going? How was the transistor developed? Who were D. W. Griffith, John Muir, Jim Thorpe, Norman Thomas?

Relation. To what extent do fashion designers dictate clothing styles? How can stamp collecting increase one's knowledge of history and geography? Are professional sports big businesses and as such subject to antitrust laws? Should athletes be allowed to form unions and bargain collectively? Should amateur filmmakers be subsidized by the government? Is astrology a science, a religion, or what?

Topical controversy   Still other research projects find their origins in the much-discussed issues of the day, those that nearly everyone has formed opinions about. You may want to select a better-known current issue to research so that your opinions about it will be based on knowledge. Some areas of controversy you might want to investigate:

Pollution of the environment.   What are the major pollutants of the environment? What are the short- or long-term effects of a certain pollutant? How does pollution relate to technology, progress, politics, education?

Overpopulation.   What is overpopulation? What can be done to stabilize the population? How are overpopulation and pollution related? How does overpopulation relate to entrenched values about the family? Where do the rights of society end and the rights of individuals and of families begin?

War, the draft, and foreign policy.   How did we get involved in Indochina? Will there be more Vietnams? How does the draft lottery compare with other systems of induction? What have we learned, or failed to learn, from Vietnam?

Race and poverty.   Is America a racist country? Is discrimination as widespread now as in the past? Why do we still have poverty in the midst of such apparent affluence? Is the wealth of the nation more evenly distributed now than in the past? Should it be more evenly distributed?

The cities.   What can be done to make our cities more liveable? Is the city obsolete? What alternatives to city living have been proposed? How are conditions in the cities related to such matters as mental illness, crime, and racial unrest?

Crime, the courts, and law and order.   Why is our crime rate so high? Where does one draw the line between police protection and police suppression? How does crime relate to poverty, education, age, personality?

Women's rights.   To what extent is femininity biologically determined and to what extent is it culturally determined? If women ever become fully liberated to work and pursue careers as men do, what will become of traditional male-female relationships, and what will become of the family structure as we know it?

Topics based on reading assignments   Many students choose research topics that are mentioned in assigned chapters, essays, stories, or poems they found interesting. The goal usually is to follow up on that provocative paragraph in the assigned essay about how only rats and men kill their own species, or to read more stories like the one about the homecoming soldier who couldn't fit in as well as he could before going to war. The reading selection should generate a research question: Why does man kill his own species? How does combat affect one's view of life?

Writing the question

Now that you have glimpsed some possible research topics and some strategies for pursuing these topics, you'll want to write your own question. You may not care to frame your question in any of the strategies of inquiry—classification, cause and effect, relation—this chapter has mentioned. You may, for instance, simply ask, "What is Zen Buddhism?" or "Who was Malcolm X?" or "Should capital punishment be abolished?" But, as we have seen, certain topics often pair well with certain strategies of inquiry. Examples:

Topic: Zen Buddhism.
Possible strategies for research questions:
1. *Comparison:* How does Zen compare with other types of Buddhism?
2. *Itemization:* What are the major features of Zen Buddhism?
3. *Relation:* How does Zen Buddhism relate to Eastern thought in general?

Topic: Malcolm X.
Possible strategies for research questions:
1. *Cause and effect:* What impact, if any, did Malcolm X's ideas have on the civil rights movement of the late sixties?
2. *Time:* How did Malcolm X modify his views on race relations?

Topic: Capital punishment.
Possible strategies for research questions:
1. *Time:* How have ideas about crime and punishment changed in the past few decades?
2. *Deduction:* What are the moral arguments against capital punishment?
3. *Relation:* What is the connection between capital punishment and the crime rate?

Restricting the inquiry You could run into trouble if your research question deals with a topic that is too broad to research well in the time you have. The broader the topic, the more you must read to become informed. If you haven't the time to read everything suggested by a broad topic, your conclusions, and your later paper, could lack depth and insight. Consider this question:

How can the environment be improved?

"Environment" suggests water, air, land, mountains, forests, cities; "improved" suggests cleaning up, beautifying, restoring, making liveable, preserving. Any one of these aspects could keep a researcher busy for weeks. Revised questions:

1. How can our waterways be made cleaner?
2. How can our recreational land be preserved?
3. What alternatives to the automobile might city dwellers consider?

Additional examples of restricting too-broad research questions:

Original question: How does the Catholic Church need to reform?

Revisions: Should the Church change its stand on birth control? Should priests be allowed to marry?

Original question: What are the problems facing senior citizens?

Revisions: Do the elderly receive adequate medical care? What problems arise when people retire earlier and live longer?

Some research questions, rather than dealing in broad topics, ask too much. Often a long, strungalong question is really two or three questions punctuated as one. Any one of the questions could develop into full-blown research projects. Examples:

Original question: What is the so-called "new morality," who practices it, and how has it affected religious values as well as interpersonal relationships?

Separate questions:

1. What is the new morality?
2. Among which types of people is the "new morality" popular?
3. How has the "new morality" affected the religious values of those who practice it?
4. What kind of relationships are formed between persons who practice the "new morality"?

Original question: What are the major political, social, and economic causes of crime?

Separate questions:

1. What are the major political causes of crime?
2. What are the major social causes of crime?
3. What are the major economic causes of crime?

But there are two dangers in restricting your inquiry too much or asking too little. First, restricting your inquiry too much may make it difficult to find materials to read. While there are numerous books and articles written about crime in general, there are obviously fewer materials available about just the political causes of crime. If you have trouble finding materials bearing on a restricted topic, you may have to broaden it somewhat to find enough materials to make your efforts worthwhile. Second, you could cheat yourself by restricting your inquiry too much. If you don't know very much about a particular topic you want to research, you may prefer to ask a rather general question that will purposely lead you into several related fields. Such general readings could provide you with valuable breadth. After acquiring this breadth, you may want to ask a new question more narrowly focused on a specific aspect of the topic. The goal is to strike a balance between asking a question that is so broad as to be a poor guide for reading and asking a question that is so narrow in scope as to deny you the big picture.

Clarity and completeness Your question won't serve you well unless it is clear and complete. It is possible, of course, that even if your question is hard for someone else to follow, *you* may know perfectly well what you are after. But often an unclear or incomplete question means unclear, incomplete thinking. The value of writing a readable question is the demand it places on clear, complete thinking. Here are some hard-to-follow questions and possible revisions:

> *Original question:* What is the difference between love and quarreling?

What does the researcher mean? Obviously love and quarreling are different. Perhaps the researcher doesn't really want to compare love and quarreling as much as explore effects:

> *Revision:* How does quarreling enhance love and how does it weaken it?

Another example:

> *Original question:* Is the family out of date for the mentally ill?

Does the researcher mean the mentally ill shouldn't have families of their own, or that families can no longer take care of the mentally ill? Suppose the latter:

> *Revision:* What are the relative responsibilities of the family and of society in caring for the mentally ill?

Worthwhile inquiry "Worthwhile" here means that your question will help you learn something you didn't know before and will give you a chance to explore something you are truly interested in as well. Don't pose a question whose answer you already know, unless you mean to read with an open mind to test your hunches. But a trite question often contains hidden questions that can lead to worthwhile research.

Trite question: Is speeding dangerous?

Revision: How can high-speed driving be made safer?

Trite question: Should we preserve our natural resources?

Revision: What substitutes have been found or developed for such natural resources as oil and metals?

Also, make sure your question, however original or interesting to you, can be answered by reading. Reading is not the only way to inform one's self. Many people pose worthwhile questions that are answered by simply thinking, or by living, traveling, working, growing up, or consulting other people. For instance, the student who wants to know which religious denomination, if any, he should affiliate with might read in the area of religion, or he might spend his time attending different churches and talking to pastors, friends, or relatives. If you feel your readings are not really answering your question, you may want to pose a different question on the same topic or find a new topic and a new question—one you might answer by reading on your own.

Finally, your question may not occur to you until after you have begun your readings. Many students feel they don't know enough about their topics to ask satisfactory questions. If you feel this way, you may want to browse through a book or two on your topic before posing your research question.

AFTERCHAPTER

The Longer Paper[1]

Write a research question based on a topic of your choice. Make sure the topic is restricted and the question is clear and complete. Make sure, too, your question will result in worthwhile reading.

Activities

1. For class discussion: What are some major topics for research not mentioned in this chapter?
2. Match any five topics below with an appropriate research strategy and write a research question for each. Example:

   Topic: Race

   Strategy: Time

   Question: How did the civil rights movement change during the 1960s?

---

[1]Beginning with this chapter and continuing through Chapter 9, a number of specific "step" assignments will be described to help you complete a longer (above, say, seven pages) research paper.

TOPICS	RESEARCH STRATEGIES
A. The working mother.	1. Itemization.
B. A "good" job.	2. Classification.
C. Automation.	3. Comparison.
D. Premarital sex.	4. Cause and effect.
E. Traffic congestion.	5. Problem and solution.
F. Sports.	6. Time.
G. Insecurity.	7. Deduction.
H. Street crime.	8. Relation.
I. Forest fires.	
J. Family problems.	
K. Popular music.	
L. Overpopulation.	
M. Religion.	
N. Success on the job.	
O. Topics of your choice.	

3. Rewrite each of the following research questions to restrict its range of inquiry. Example:
   Question: What is the relationship between science and religion?
   Revision: What is the relationship between the theory of evolution and the book of Genesis?
   a. What does the younger generation want?
   b. How can crime be reduced?
   c. What causes divorce?
   d. What are the causes of pollution and its effects and why can't we solve the problem?
   e. What makes people violent?

4. Rewrite each of the following trite questions so as to aim at more challenging aspects of the topic. Example:
   Question: Have American Indians been mistreated?
   Revision: How does the plight of the American Indian compare with the plight of other minority groups?
   a. Does automation put people out of work?
   b. Is cigaret smoking harmful?
   c. Should politicians be honest?
   d. What is the Catholic stand on birth control?
   e. Should everyone go to college who can benefit?

4

Locating Materials To Read

Few institutions of Western civilization are as gloomy, unfriendly, intimidating, and stuffy as libraries. The seats are hard, the lighting is usually poor, the restrictions on smoking, eating, and talking are mostly silly, and the books, magazines, and other materials are stored away with a stone-age ignorance of modern technological retrieval systems.

Some people feel libraries should be run by computers and high-speed copying machines so that instead of checking out something, you can have what you want printed out at low cost. Other people feel libraries could stand a little rock music or jazz piped in here and there. An espresso urn and a beer tap or two might also help. So might pop posters alongside those weary busts of Galileo, Newton, and Shakespeare. All this amid bright cushions and flowered hammocks where patrons can throw off their shoes, stretch out, and read or just think.

Like so many things, libraries are changing, and for the better.[1] For the time being, however, you'll have to track down your books and materials on foot. This chapter explains, in a general way, how to get around your college library to find the materials you need to answer the question you have chosen to look into for your research project. Later on in the chapter, we will consider some sources beyond your college library that might offer information you can use.

Locating books The *card catalog* is the best place to begin your search for books. Most books are represented by at least three cards in the card catalog—a subject card, an author card, and a title card. Sample subject card:

---

[1]My county library now allows smoking in the reference room. (Historically, the prohibition on smoking in libraries stems less from a fear of fire than from puritanical hangups about desecrating holy places: you can't smoke in libraries for the same reasons you can't smoke in church.) When it was discovered that most patrons of the San Francisco public library were over thirty, the library's staff started offering light shows and rock concerts to attract younger patrons.

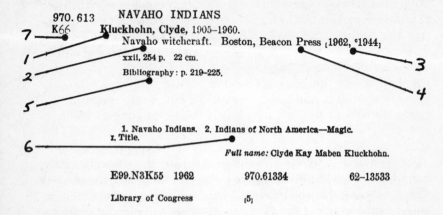

1. Navaho Indians. 2. Indians of North America—Magic.
ɪ. Title.

E99.N3K55 1962   970.61334   62-13533

Library of Congress   ₍5₎

"NAVAHO INDIANS" is the subject under which this card was filed. Like all catalog cards, this card gives you a lot of information:

1. Author: Clyde Kluckhohn.
2. Title: *Navajo Witchcraft.*
3. Year of Publication: 1962; first copyrighted in 1944.
4. Publisher: Beacon Press.
5. Bibliography: found on pages 219-225.
6. Cross references: an identical card is filed under "Indians of North America—Magic."
7. Call number: 970.613/K66

Some of this information can be very useful. A book's *year of publication* may not matter much for subjects like Navajo witchcraft, but obviously you don't want to waste time tracking down an old book if your research question deals with a contemporary, fast-moving issue—unless you have a hunch the book may be noteworthy for explaining useful principles or providing important background information.

Catalog cards can also lead you to *bibliographies* in books. These bibliographies can provide you with a wealth of names and titles to follow up in the card catalog.

Cross references tell you where identical cards have been filed in the card catalog under different but related subjects. Browsing through these related subject cards could uncover additional useful books.

Call numbers for books, for example, 970.613/K66, are entered in the upper lefthand corner of catalog cards. Books, as you know, are kept in *the stacks,* shelved according to call numbers. If you know how call numbers work and which stacks correspond to which call numbers, you can climb the right number of stairs or make the right number of turns to find your books. However, only librarians bother to learn the system on which call numbers are based; the rest of us find our books through one of two expedients: we consult a big sign that explains where books bearing certain call numbers are found, or we ask a librarian. These methods usually place us within a stack or two of what we want. When we do finally blunder across the shelf where the book we want should be, the book is usually gone—lost, stolen, mutilated, or checked out. So we return to the card catalog and start all over again. Sorry, but this is the best system our advanced technological civilization has yet devised for retrieving books.

While standing before a shelf where a book should be but isn't, don't fail to browse through other nearby books. Stack-browsing in the vicinity of books you want is often a better way to find pertinent books than thumbing through the card catalog. In some libraries, students aren't allowed to browse in the stacks at all, unless they are honors students or graduate students. If they are neither, they have to fill out detailed slips for books and give them to clerks to run down. This often lengthy procedure is meant, apparently, to discourage just-average students from checking out too many books and possibly becoming better students.

Locating magazine articles   Librarians like to make a distinction between periodicals and magazines. It gives them something to learn in graduate school. In most instances, however, periodical means magazine; periodical literature means magazine articles.

Indexes to periodical literature (magazine articles) are available for use in the reference room of the library. These indexes give you about the same information for magazine articles as the card file gives you for books: subject, author, title of article, name of magazine, page numbers, and date of publication. The most useful index of this type, probably, is the *Reader's Guide to Periodical Literature.* This is a long row of thick books set out on a table in the reference room. The *Reader's Guide* lists articles by both author and subject for a great many magazines going back for decades. Sample entries from the *Reader's Guide* appear on page 36.

Hard to follow? Let's translate:
COLLEGE libraries
"COLLEGE" is the subject, "libraries" is a major heading under "COLLEGE."

Automation
"Automation" is a minor heading under "COLLEGE—libraries."
Automating Columbia's libraries. il
Sch & Soc 97:276+ Sum '69

"Automating Columbia's libraries" is the title of one article. "Il" means the article is illustrated. "Sch & Soc" stands for the name of the magazine, in this case *School and Society.* "97:276+" means volume number 97, page 276 plus a few more pages in the back of the magazine. "Sum '69" refers to the summer issue of 1969. Fortunately, these abbreviations and others are explained in the first few pages of all volumes of the *Reader's Guide.*

There are several other useful indexes to magazine articles which your library may or may not carry. None of them is as comprehensive as the *Reader's Guide. Poole's Index,* for instance, covers nineteenth-century magazines, if these are what you need. Two of the more specialized indexes are the *Social Science and Humanities Index* and the *Education Index.* Other indexes list magazine articles in the fields of business, engineering, music, law, and literature.

To find out what magazines your library carries, go to the *periodical file.* This is usually located in the reference room. The periodical file will tell you when your library started taking whatever magazine you are interested in. It will also give you the call number of the magazine. Magazines are bound in hardcover volumes each year and stored in the stacks like other books. Very recent issues of magazines are stored unbound somewhere in the reference room, often hidden away as if to imply you are untrustworthy. Forget about getting your hands on magazines about a year old. These are usually "at the bindery" to be sewn into single volumes, and for mysterious reasons this job takes months. It is usually forbidden to take any magazine, bound or unbound, out of the library.

Many libraries have converted to a system of photographing magazines on microfilm. The microfilm is then viewed on a microfilm reader, which occasionally can be focused well enough to read.

Locating newspaper stories The most widely available index to newspaper stories is the *New York Times Index,* also found in the reference room. It treats only the *New York Times,* which your library may carry on microfilm. If your college doesn't subscribe to the *New York Times,* you can still use the *New York Times Index* to find stories in back issues of your local newspaper. The date of a story of national interest listed in the *Index* will lead you to a similar story your local newspaper printed on the same day. If your college library doesn't keep back issues of your local newspaper, visit the newspaper's office and ask to see the issue you want.

Another way to locate pertinent newspaper stories is to read a newspaper every day during the period you have budgeted for research. It is especially important to read newspapers if your research topic is very current. If you can't read a newspaper daily, you might want to set aside some time to visit your library and thumb through a number of recent newspapers to find stories pertaining to your research question.

Locating reference works   The reference room of your library contains a number of reference works you may find useful:

Bibliographies are lists of sources—books, magazine articles, pamphlets, and so forth—on a single subject. The reference room houses a number of book-length bibliographies you may want to look into: *Guide to Historical Literature, Biography Index, Books in Print, Bibliographic Index,* and, for overkill, an *Index to Indexes.*

Encyclopedias are often good places to begin research. Encyclopedias, of course, provide concise overviews of topics, explanations, useful facts, and brief biographies of famous people. Longer entries usually conclude with bibliographies of well-known pertinent books.

Other useful reference works may be found in the reference room. Special encyclopedias deal with specific subjects: the social sciences, religion, literature, music, science, and so forth. These special encyclopedias contain valuable data, descriptions, definitions, and biographies. Yearbooks and almanacs such as the *Statistical Abstract of the United States* can provide you with up-to-date statistics on a great number of subjects. A few afternoons in the reference room of your library can yield much valuable information you might not find elsewhere.

Locating literary material   If you plan to read poems, stories, and the like, use the card catalog to locate books by the writers you are interested in. Thumb through both author and subject cards. If you wish to find critical commentary about a well-known writer, look for subject cards that bear the writer's name. For instance, "Hemingway, Ernest," as a subject, should lead you to critical books by people like Phillip Young and Carlos Baker, two experts on Hemingway. The reference room contains several useful literary indexes and reference tools. Examples: *Subject Index to Poetry, Articles on American Literature Appearing in Current Periodicals, Concise Dictionary of American Literature, Oxford Companion to American Literature.* Also, consult your English teacher for additional names, titles, and strategies for locating literary material.

Locating a variety of materials   A research question is sometimes best answered after reading a variety of materials that answer the question from different points of view. For instance, to answer the question, "Should the Catholic Church modify its position on birth control?" a student might consider reading comments by priests and theologians, philosophers, population experts, marriage counselors, social workers, physicians, and parents themselves. Arguments for and against birth control by the clergy would probably dominate the student's reading, but he should not exclude opinions by other persons who have some claim to authority about the subject of birth control. Variety of this kind could lend the finished paper, whatever its conclusions, a sense of relatedness and perspective.

To locate a variety of materials, make a list of topics related in various ways to the topic of your research question. Then use the card catalog, the *Reader's Guide,* and other locator devices to find materials related to your research topic. Example:

Research topic: birth control.

Related topics: Catholic Church, theology, religion, overpopulation, population, marriage, marital problems, social problems, abortion, contraception, public health, family life, underdeveloped countries, poverty.

The greater the number of related topics you can think of, the more luck you'll have in locating a variety of materials.

Subordinating your topic to subjects listed in locator devices Some students who claim they can't find materials expect too much of locator devices. The card file and the *Reader's Guide* can't possibly list all possible subjects. Instead, they must deal with relatively broad subjects. You will have to use a little imagination and subordinate the specific topic your question deals with to broader subjects listed in locator devices. You will have to anticipate what broader subjects in locator devices your research topic falls under. Examples:

Specific topics for research questions	*Possible broader subjects in locator devices*
1. The use of gas in Vietnam.	Warfare, Gas Warfare, Biochemical Warfare, Weaponry, Vietnam, War.
2. Political commercials on TV.	Politics, Elections, Communications, Media, TV, Advertising, Public Opinion, Propaganda, Political Campaigns.
3. The preservation of endangered species.	Wildlife, Animals, Extinct Species, Endangered Species, Ecology, Conservation, Zoos, Animal Reserves, Hunting, Trapping, Fur Industry.

Librarians This chapter makes no claim to completeness. It aims to describe a few useful procedures for locating materials rather than provide a detailed account of how libraries are organized. I hope you will take steps to help yourself and learn what you have to in order to track down the materials you need. One important step you should take is to discuss your research question, and the materials you think you need, with a librarian.

Librarians are actually real people. They like to walk among flowers and scrunch up their toes in grass and run along the beach with their dogs and children. Unlike the fish in Mammouth Cove, librarians have real eyes that blink when they emerge from darkness into sunlight. And like all people, librarians want to feel useful and appreciated. Instead of spending their time Scotch-taping torn pages and telling patrons to be quiet, they would rather help patrons find the materials they need. Most librarians, too, are very well educated and have a wide range of interests and knowledge. They can suggest names, titles, strategies. They can also answer the many specific questions you may have about such matters as call numbers, locations of books and magazines, reference works you can use, the library's policy for reserving books—questions this chapter cannot take up without growing overlong.

Beyond your college library

In your search for materials, don't overlook these sources:

Other libraries in your area Perhaps there are other colleges and universities in your area with libraries larger than your college library. Books unavailable in your college library might be found in these other libraries. Because you will not possess a library card for these other college libraries, you will not, of course, receive the full range of services; but usually no one will mind (or know) if you browse or sit and take notes. Your own college library may also have interlibrary borrowing agreements with these libraries. Check on this.

Don't overlook the larger city and county libraries, which often are quite good. City libraries have different patrons than college libraries; the books they want are not always books students want. Books that seem always to be checked out from your college library might await you in your city library.

Bookstores The so-called paperback revolution in publishing has made it possible to reprint at relatively low cost a great number of excellent books written by recognized experts. Some of these books are classics that date back for decades or even centuries; others are quite recent and in fact may be more up to date than the books in your library. Many research projects depend on one or two key books, and often these books are available in paperback. The student who owns these books does not have to worry about locating them in the library or getting them back before the due date. He also finds note-taking greatly simplified because he always has his books at hand for reference at every step of research.

You may find some bookstore clerks nearly as knowledgeable as librarians, and perhaps even more eager to help you. If you spend a few minutes discussing your research question with a clerk, he may lead you to several books you can use. Some students find that the few dollars they spend on a key paperback book or two are more than offset by the time and effort they save by not having to retrieve these books from libraries.

Agencies and organizations If your research question deals with some aspect of the law or government, you might drop by certain offices of government where literature is made available to the public. In California, for instance, county government offices carry a wide range of pamphlets on such subjects as air pollution, welfare, crime, safety, and land management. Both state and federal governments publish an enormous variety of materials on virtually all subjects.

Many nongovernmental organizations in your city distribute worthwhile literature. Your local American Cancer Society will tell you all about smoking. If you have a chapter of the American Civil Liberties Union in your city, you can pick up information on constitutional rights and their relation to topical issues. Labor union headquarters often give out information on employment, automation, the cost of living, and so forth.

Resource people Don't fail to check with your teacher to see if he can suggest books and other materials you can use. You might also visit other teachers who teach subjects more directly related to your research subject. If your research question is about war, see a political science or history teacher. If about the effects of drug use, see a health education teacher or a psychology teacher. If ecology, see a biologist or geographer. Knowing books in their field is the business of these teachers. Visit them during their office hours and be brief. It helps if you have taken, or are currently taking, their courses and have impressed them by displaying at least a mild interest in the subjects they teach.

Also, plan to see a nonteaching expert or two in a field your research project touches on. These people can give you valuable firsthand information and expert opinion, as well as titles of books to look into and names to follow up. If you are doing a paper on job opportunities for psychology majors, see a practicing psychologist. If a paper on religion, see a priest, rabbi, or minister. If urban development, see a city planner. If prostitution—well, suit yourself.

Writing away for materials   A great many organizations and interest groups publish materials you can obtain through the mails, free for the asking. You can, for instance, get materials on conservation from both the Sierra Club and Georgia-Pacific, a wood products company. The National Safety Council will mail you literature on highway safety and so will the Goodyear Tire and Rubber Company. The media are your best source for learning about these giveaways. Note ads that say, "Write for free brochure."

Two dangers in writing for literature: First, time. You must write early and allow several weeks for delivery so you can work the literature into the writing of your paper before the due date. Second, treatment. Most of the material you get from these outfits is written by public relations men to further the cause, financial or otherwise, of the organizations they represent. So do not read this literature uncritically. Still, facts are facts, and even public relations men deserve a fair hearing. The shrewd researcher may even use the propaganda he gets in the mail to make a certain point: You may decide an oil company's slick pamphlet about how it eased Eskimos into the modern world obscures basic issues about tribal dignity.

There is nothing wrong with gathering materials from sources outside your college library, but you'll probably discover that your library remains your best source of responsible material , and, in the end, the one easiest to work with.

AFTERCHAPTER

The Longer Paper

Make a list of books, magazine articles, and other materials you feel will be useful for answering your research question. Use the card file, the *Reader's Guide,* reference works, and librarians. Make your list rather long and chancy: You won't be sure all the materials you list will be pertinent, but the longer your list, the better your chances for finding useful materials. Obtain additional reading material from bookstores, agencies, and so forth in your community. Try to interview an expert, if you feel he might be helpful.

Activities

1. Take a librarian to lunch.
2. If activity 1 proves difficult, speak with a librarian for five minutes or so about either your research question or how to find materials to read to answer it.

3. For each research topic below, supply four related or broader subjects that might be listed in locator devices. For examples, see pages 00 and 00. Research topics:
   A. Modern theories about the relationship of man to God.
   B. Using TV to teach students history.
   C. Juvenile delinquency among suburban middle-class youths.
   D. Motorcycle racing.
   E. Compact computers for the home.
   F. Establishing a chain of "youth hotels" for students who travel in the summer.

4. Spend ten or fifteen minutes thumbing through the card file to get the feel of it. Note how cards are posted by subject, author, and title.

5. Use the card file to find *two* books on *each* of the following research questions:
   A. What steps has the federal government taken to halt pollution?
   B. What have modern theologians written about the relationship of man to God?
   C. Who was John Muir?
   D. What are the job opportunities for recent college graduates who majored in the liberal arts (English, history, art, etc.)?

6. Spend ten minutes or so thumbing through the *Reader's Guide* to get the feel of it. Use the key found in the opening pages of each volume to figure out the abbreviations of the entries.

7. Use the *Reader's Guide* to locate two magazine articles on *each* of the following topics:
   A. What has Detroit done recently to make cars safer?
   B. What has been the effect of prolonged strikes on the nation's economy?
   C. How does filmmaking in Communist countries compare with filmmaking in the United States?
   D. How is television being used in schools?

8. Spend a half hour in the reference room of your library and try to familiarize yourself with as many useful reference works as possible. You be the judge as to what is "useful."

9. Consult encyclopedias and other reference works to answer these questions:
   A. Why do earthquakes occur frequently in regions that ring the Pacific Ocean?
   B. Which state leads in the production of cotton?
   C. Which national park is visited by the greatest number of tourists?
   D. What is titanium?
   E. What was the median income of U.S. families last year?

10. Visit a trade bookstore in your town. Ask a clerk to recommend two paperback books that could help you answer your research question. Break down and buy one.

5
Reading and Note-taking

Of all the arts of research, probably none is more crucial yet more difficult to practice than effective reading. Reading to answer a research question is a solitary, private activity. You are on your own with little more to guide you than a question and a stack of materials. No teacher stands nearby to check your "work"; for reading, unlike writing, is interior and inaccessible to others. All your teacher can do is look at your notes, but he can't look at your reading itself. He can't get in your head to follow your reading and suggest: "Read this passage closer. Skip that passage." Only you can make the important decisions about what to read and what not to read. But this chapter might help you. It discusses, first, *how* you might read more efficiently to sample a variety of materials and, second, *what* kinds of materials you might read and take notes on. The chapter closes with some suggestions for taking notes.

Efficient reading

How much you read isn't simply a matter of how much time you have; it also depends on how well you use your time. You can usually save time and learn more if you practice the techniques of skimming and scanning, two types of reading meant to help you sample a wide range of material.

Skimming is a type of "speed reading" intended to give you broad outlines and general ideas. You don't read every paragraph or even every page when you skim. Instead you glance at:

Introductions: the first several paragraphs of an article or a chapter; the preface and table of contents of a book; most of the first chapter of a book.

Typographical cues: chapter and subchapter titles, italics, boldface print.

First sentences of paragraphs: not all paragraphs, but rather those that begin major sections of a chapter or an article.

Conclusions: last paragraphs of major sections; last paragraphs of articles and chapters; last chapters of books.

You can skim an article or a chapter in a matter of minutes, a book in ten or fifteen minutes. You skim to answer two questions:

1. Will this work provide me with important background information relating to my research question?
2. Does this work contain certain passages that can help me answer my research question?

Scanning is follow-up reading. The purpose of skimming is to get enough general information about the selection to determine if you want to spend any more time with it. If you do, you go back and scan those passages you found most useful. Scanning is a closer, slower type of reading than skimming. Like skimming, you needn't read everything when you scan. You can often skip whole paragraphs and pages. But what you do read you read carefully.

Rapid skimming followed by selective, intensive scanning lets you use your time better. You can look into a large number of books and articles this way because you seldom read anything in its entirety. Instead you read just a paragraph of one article, a page from another, perhaps only a chapter or two from a book. You read only what you need to read to find either pertinent background information or specific information related to your research question. You ignore, or spend less time with, everything else.

But skimming and scanning have their disadvantages. While they are useful for answering specific questions and getting into a wide variety of material, they do tend to fragment ideas and interfere with your enjoyment in following a writer's development of thought. If skimming and scanning and jumping around give you a headache, then perhaps you'll want to read slowly and sequentially, the way you are used to. If you want to spend ten days rather than ten minutes on a certain book, then do it. Above all, find a way to read that will help you learn most and enjoy your research. At the same time be practical. Make sure your resistance to speed-reading techniques will not result in failing to inform yourself and come to conclusions. The shrewd researcher understands and practices all these types of reading.

Reading for background

Your research will be more enjoyable and your findings clearer if you first gather some general background information about your chosen topic before reading more narrowly to answer your specific research question.

For instance, what background information might be helpful for answering this question?

What impact did the advent of sound in 1927 have on the later development of film art?

Here is a pertinent excerpt from a book about the history of motion pictures:

Until about 1912 inventors persisted in their efforts to join together sound and visuals, going so far as to run endless belts from the projector motor through the entire length of the theater to a phonograph installed behind the screen. But they soon discovered, as houses continued to grow larger, that the problem was one not merely of synchronization but of amplification as well. The ordinary talking machine simply could not produce the volume of sound required to fill an entire auditorium.

The solution lay in the silenium tube, the so-called "audion amplifier" developed by Lee De Forest shortly before World War I. With it, volume could be controlled, stepped up. Of great importance in long-distance telephone and telegraph experiments, it was basic to the development of the infant radio industry and the talking picture. De Forest sold his amplification patents to Bell Telephone; but soon after the war he began to devote his attention to the problem of sound and films, choosing an entirely new approach. Hitherto, the sound had always been separated from the film strip, a phonograph record to be played along with the picture. De Forest saw that this presented strong disadvantages. The loss of a few frames of film through a break or a splice would throw the whole remaining reel out of synchronization with its accompanying sound, while a broken record could wreck an entire show. In addition, the mechanics of obtaining and maintaining a synchronization between the sound and the image became infinitely more complicated when the two were handled on separate machines.

To circumvent this, De Forest developed a method of photographing sound directly on the film itself, recording it in fine striations of grays and blacks along one edge of the strip. Vibrations caught by the microphone broke the current of a photo-electric cell; the resulting fluctuations of light and dark, photographed on motion-picture film, gave back the original sound impulses when passed around another photo-electric cell in the sound head of the projector.

This passage, then, provides the researcher a *historical perspective* for his research topic. The passage also gives important *technical information* bearing on the research topic. Additional background reading might touch on:

Prominent figures. D. W. Griffith and Sergei Eisenstein were important names in the development of film art.

Crucial issues and better-known pros and cons. To this day filmmakers do not agree on the role sound should play in movies.

Crucial facts and recent developments. Studio executives, rather than filmmakers, promoted sound to increase profits. More recently, filmmakers are using popular music rather than dialogue or natural sound to accompany certain scenes.

What kind of background material you read depends, of course, on the nature of your research topic and how much you feel you need to know about it. Another example:

> *Research question:* What is the connection between the so-called military-industrial complex and our system of college education?
>
> *Background reading:*
>
> *The historical perspective:* Cold war politics since World War II; Eisenhower's famous "farewell address" about the military-industrial complex; the rise of defense-related research in the universities.
>
> *Crucial issues and better-known pros and cons:* Should the military be cut back? Should the universities engage in defense-related research?
>
> *Crucial facts and recent developments:* The financial crisis facing higher education; the disenchantment of some students with large institutions, military and educational.

Background reading is also a good way to test your interests. You may decide, after looking into a few books or articles, that either the topic or the question you chose is not right for you. You may elect to abandon the topic and choose another, or you may want to pose a new question based on the same topic. As noted in an earlier chapter, some students begin their background reading with no definite question at all. They feel they don't know enough about their topic to ask satisfactory questions. So they read broadly in a chosen topic to learn enough to ask informed, useful questions.

Reading to answer the research question

The discussion below treats seven types of reading material you might look into to answer your research question: (1) facts and statistics, (2) inferences, (3) studies and experiments, (4) examples or case studies, (5) expert opinion, (6) related topics and general principles, and (7) literary material.

Facts and statistics   Be alert for pertinent facts and statistics that come up in the materials you read. Facts are statements that reveal who, what, where, or when. Whatever the statement is about can be checked out and verified by anyone. Statistics deal in numbers and quantities. They show how many, how much, how often. Statistics are often found in the form of tables or charts in reference works and appendixes, or they may be worked into the running commentary of a writer. Below is a table followed by a sample commentary with facts and statistics:

Obligations by the Department of Defense for Research and Development at 100 Universities and Colleges Receiving the Largest Amounts, 1966
(Dollar Amounts in Thousands)

INSTITUTION NAME	STATE	RANK	DEPT. OF DEFENSE
Mass. Inst. of Technology	Mass.	1	35,078
Stanford University	Cal.	2	21,930
University of Michigan	Mich.	3	21,579
Columbia University	N.Y.	4	14,829
University of Illinois	Ill.	5	14,075
U. of Cal. Los Angeles	Cal.	6	11,492
University of Pennsylvania	Pa.	7	8,510
Cornell University	N.Y.	8	8,220
University of Texas	Texas	9	6,145
Harvard University	Mass.	10	5,881
U. of Cal. Berkeley	Cal.	11	5,399
University of Denver	Colo.	12	5,307
University of Chicago	Ill.	13	5,077
Syracuse University	N.Y.	14	5,045
Brown University	R.I.	15	4,790
New York University	N.Y.	16	4,715
Northwestern University	Ill.	17	4,714
Ohio State University	Ohio	18	4,238
California Inst. of Tech.	Cal.	19	3,801
Johns Hopkins University	Md.	20	3,791
Purdue University	Ind.	21	3,767
University of Dayton	Ohio	22	3,641
Princeton University	N.J.	23	3,602
George Washington University	D.C.	24	3,433
University of Maryland	Md.	25	3,364
Duke University	N.C.	26	3,141
Carnegie Inst. Technology	Pa.	27	2,874
University of Pittsburgh	Pa.	28	2,715
Washington University	Md.	29	2,549
Polytechnic Inst. Brooklyn	N.Y.	30	2,487
Pennsylvania State University	Pa.	31	2,364
University of N.C. at Chapel Hill	N.C.	32	2,234

ARMY	NAVY	AIR FORCE	DEFENSE AGENCY	DEPT. WIDE FUNDS
5,485	9,672	17,542	2,379	0
5,951	8,174	5,126	2,679	0
10,868	1,560	7,314	1,837	0
1,138	8,935	4,756	0	0
6,419	2,391	3,141	2,071	53
1,348	9,337	807	0	0
4,276	802	932	2,500	0
2,785	838	2,198	2,376	23
669	4,214	1,262	0	0
2,109	1,445	1,035	1,292	0
1,055	2,380	1,676	253	35
424	163	4,696	24	0
1,937	488	1,487	1,165	0
1,269	3,066	710	0	0
1,984	614	544	1,648	0
1,765	1,451	1,499	0	0
1,769	869	258	1,818	0
360	180	3,523	0	175
789	2,075	937	0	0
1,450	910	1,381	0	50
1,544	474	804	945	0
0	50	3,591	0	0
843	1,857	885	17	0
358	3,042	33	0	0
2,140	250	399	536	39
2,672	145	324	0	0
1,754	947	173	0	0
1,574	443	620	0	78
1,381	20	148	1,000	0
153	1,323	1,011	0	0
967	509	868	0	20
1,222	110	288	634	0

Another striking example of vested interests is the defense establishment's impact upon the state of Georgia which doesn't even rank in the first ten of the states in total funds received from the Department of Defense. Georgia has thirteen major military installations headed by the vast reservation at Ft. Benning, home of some 53,000 Army troops. The giant Lockheed-Georgia plant outside of Atlanta builds the C-5A Galaxy as well as the C-130 and C-141 military transports. It pours a $6 million weekly payroll into the local economy; Lockheed and other Georgia-based defense firms received $964 million in prime military contracts during 1968. In addition military personnel in Georgia received $650 million in pay and allowances while 45,400 civilian employees at military installations received $337 million in salaries during 1968. Georgia also has 500,000 veterans receiving $280 million in benefits. If such defense-related activities as NASA, the Atomic Energy Commission, and the Corps of Engineers' projects working in Georgia during 1968 are added, total defense-related money going into the state annually amounts to about $2.3 billion.

Inferences　You can use the facts and statistics you discover in two ways: (1) You can draw your own conclusions from them, or (2) you can note the conclusions drawn by the writers who cite them. Conclusions drawn from facts and statistics are called *inferences.* Inferences are never one hundred percent certain, although their certainty is sometimes increased as writers present more facts and statistics in support of their inferences. The following passage assembles some facts and statistics to support the inference that our major universities have become partners or even captives of those who shape U.S. foreign policy:

In a good many instances the liaisons between the defense agencies and the universities were accomplished through the federal contract research centers. There are forty-seven of them; the centers do $1.2 billion worth of research and development work annually, almost all of it sponsored by the Defense Department or the Atomic Energy Commission. Nearly half the money goes to centers managed by universities. The center idea has provided a convenient way for inveigling bright scientists into defense work. The government can pay the scientists higher wages by hiring them through universities, thereby getting around the civil service pay scales. As for the scientists themselves, they appear more distinguished to their colleagues as members of the faculty of some great university than if they were working on bomb sites in some dingy Pentagon office. And the centers give the universities a bit of prestige and a management fee. (Johns Hopkins gets $1 million annually in fees for administering the $50 million budget of the Applied Physics Laboratory.)

In theory, the government gets the best independent scientific advice in this manner, but in fact, what happens is that the major universities become first captive and then active advocates for the military and paramilitary agencies of government in order to get more money for research.

Studies and experiments   Occasionally you will run across descriptions of studies and experiments that may bear on your research question. Studies and experiments are systematic attempts to relate at least two sets of data. People who conduct studies and experiments draw inferences from how sets of data relate. Here is a summary of a study that related the changing nature of certain jobs with the changing educational requirements for those jobs:

The belief that changes in employers' tastes, not changes in the nature of the work itself, are responsible for the diploma race is supported by a study of the 1960 census by John K. Folger and Charles B. Nam, "Education of the American Population."

In surveying the decade from 1950 to 1960, a time of escalating diploma requirements, Folger and Nam concluded that only 15% of the increased demand for diplomas could be accounted for by changes in the nature of work. The other 85%, they found, was the result of added diploma requirements for the same jobs.

The inference, then, was that many jobs are not as technical or complex as their degree requirements would suggest.

Examples and case studies   As you read you should also note any pertinent examples of persons, cases, situations, and the like that will help you answer your research question. These examples can often lend your finished paper a sense of being real and concrete and rescue it from the rather dry and impersonal tone that statistics can convey. Here is an account of a capable man whose appointment to a high school principalship was not confirmed, for reasons that may point up a major deficiency in our educational system:

On the rare occasions when diplomaism in education is challenged, forces in the industry mobilize like white blood cells to meet the threat. Recently, the board of education of a suburban community—Princeton, N.J.—was taught a lesson in diplomaism. The story is educational.

The high school principal had resigned, unable to cope with a school beset by racial conflict and troubled, in a less measurable sense, by the nameless malaise of white suburban youth, children of the bourgeois intelligentsia. In a rare reach of the imagination, the board decided to go outside the industry for a new principal.

They chose a local notable, Raymond F. Male. Male was a remarkable choice. He is a former mayor of Princeton who had sided with the young in generational conflicts. He is also the state commissioner of labor and industry and an expert in public administration. In the selection of Male, the school board seemed to be saying that the troubles of high school students had mostly to do with the students' relations with the world outside the walls.

But Male is not certified to be a high school principal. When his case went to the Board of Examiners, a sort of supreme court within the state's public education bureaucracy, the examiners voted, 7 to 2, that Male was not qualified to be principal of Princeton High School.

Their grounds were that he lacked a teaching certificate and 24 credit hours in school administration. The last although Male has taught public administration and holds a master's degree in the subject from Princeton University.

Writers use examples and case studies in the same way they use facts and statistics—to draw inferences. To the writer who reported Male's plight, the incident underscored some abuses of "diplomaism":

Far from fearing that Male would fail, the examiners had more reason to be afraid he would succeed as a principal—for his success would tend to undermine the barriers so carefully erected against outsiders.

The examiners' power, like that of the guilds whose interest they represent, is essentially negative. By their control of the gates, they see to it that the only people in the industry are those who have paid their respects—and their cash—to the schools of education by getting the proper diploma.

In the suburbs, guild control has the effect of keeping out creative outsiders like Male. In the cities, the effect is to keep out creative, but degreeless, ghetto people.

You can use examples as you use facts and statistics—to draw your own inferences from them or to note the inferences drawn by writers who cite examples. Make sure, however, the examples you use are truly typical; don't generalize from unusual cases. If possible, back up the inferences you draw from examples with other confirming data.

Expert opinion Opinions don't always have to be based on facts and statistics to be noteworthy. Some opinions you'll read may strike you as reasonable or illuminating or original regardless of how they are supported. These opinions may help you put into words what you only vaguely felt before, or they may present you totally new ideas to ponder.

Sometimes it matters *who* advances a seemingly unsupported opinion. Generally, experts in the field they are advancing opinions about should be regarded higher than laymen. Experts don't always have to offer as many supporting data for their views; we take it on faith that they have reasonable grounds for their beliefs. Here is a passage by a retired Marine colonel who comments on the near-holy quality of our belief about national defense and foreign policy:

THE SACRED TRINITY

The connotations of "national defense," "patriotism" and "anticommunism" must be continually evaluated in terms of the real world. They cannot be merely sacred shibboleths used by doctrinaires and demagogues to support special interests. . . .

Patriotism in its essence is simply devotion to one's country. It is not limited to ceremonies, flags, and bands—or to uniforms and warfare. . . . It includes service for the poor, the ill, and underprivileged at home as well as fighting for allies in foreign lands. Creative productivity that will benefit the nation and bring it honor and respect is just as patriotic as sitting at the trigger of an atomic missile capable of destroying distant cities. Patriotism in its martial form, however, has been extolled by the disciples of the new militarism. . . .

National defense in its literal sense means defense of the United States and the republic's sovereign islands and bases against foreign attack or seizure. . . .

Containment of communism, . . . must be weighed in terms of the real needs of national defense. We should determine whether a nation with 3.4 million men under arms and with powerful forces numbering over 1.2 million people overseas, far from American shores, is maintaining a defensive or actually an aggressive posture. . . .

The third basic creed of American militarism is *anti-communism*. . . . Many of our political, military, and editorial opinion-makers have acquired an anti-communism syndrome. They either think they see threats of Communist aggression on all sides or they dub any social or political dissent that they don't understand or they oppose as evidence of a Communist conspiracy. The military, for its part, always has to focus upon a potential enemy. Communist aggressors are the most convenient, current, and identifiable enemy. If there were no Communist bloc and no such enemy threat, the defense establishment would have to invent one. If Soviet Russia and its satellites were all constitutional monarchies with large and powerful armed forces, they would be the enemy. If Great Britain were still a major sea power, it would be considered a potential enemy by U.S. naval war planners—as was believed in 1914. So Marxist communism in itself is not the real threat to the United States: it is the *military power* evident in much of the Communist-dominated world which constitutes the presumed danger to the United States.

Occasionally, experts in one field offer perceptive opinions about another field. They bring different, often fresh perspective to fields related to their specialties. In the following passage, a Catholic priest, long interested in Church reform, brings his background to bear on the subject of required schooling:

Durkheim recognized that this ability to divide social reality into two realms was the very essence of formal religion. There are, he reasoned, religions without the supernatural and religions without gods, but none which does not subdivide the world into things and times and persons that are sacred —and others that as a consequence are profane. Durkheim's insight can be applied to the sociology of education, for school is radically divisive in a similar way.

The very existence of *obligatory* schools divides any society into two realms: some time spans and processes and treatments and professions are "academic" or "pedagogic," and others are not. The power of school thus to divide social reality has no boundaries: education becomes unworldly and the world becomes noneducational.

Since Bonhoeffer contemporary theologians have pointed to the confusions now reigning between the biblical message and institutionalized religion. They point to the experience that Christian freedom and faith usually gain from secularization. Inevitably their statements sound blasphemous to many churchmen. Unquestionably, the educational process will gain from the de-schooling of society even though this demand sounds to many schoolmen like treason to the enlightenment. But it is enlightenment itself that is now being snuffed out in the schools.

The secularization of the Christian faith depends on the dedication to it on the part of Christians rooted in the Church. In much the same way, the de-schooling of education depends on the leadership of those brought up in the schools. Their curriculum cannot serve them as an alibi for the task: each of us remains responsible for what has been made of him, even though he might not be able to do more than accept this responsibility and serve as a warning to others.

Related topics and general principles The last passage shows the value of reading about topics slightly off the main line of inquiry. Comparing your research topic with related topics often helps you discover important general principles. These general principles could prove very useful for answering your research question. In the last passage, the priest compares two large institutions, the church and the school. The passage implies that both the church and the school need to be deinstitutionalized and "secularized," that is, scaled down and made less "holy." Perhaps this general principle could be applied to both the military and the colleges.

Literary material Many topics can be explored through the close reading of literary material, such as poems and stories. Insights about human nature and the structure of society often emerge from the broader implications of poems and stories. Reading literary material requires patience and a certain willingness to generalize from particular persons, conflicts, settings, objects, and situations. Below is a passage that concludes a short story, "The Portable Phonograph," by Walter Van Tilburg Clark. The story takes place after a devastating world war that has driven what is left of mankind back to the stone age. The central character is an old professor—or rather, ex-professor: no colleges exist—who entertains three men with great civility in his crude dugout. The professor reads from great books and plays records of classical music on his portable phonograph. The guests mourn the passing of civilization and respond to the professor's priestly ministrations with a mixture of pain, longing, and appreciation. As the passage opens, the guests have just departed from the professor's dugout.

With nervous hands he lowered the piece of canvas which served as his door, and pegged it at the bottom. Then quickly and quietly, looking at the piece of canvas frequently, he slipped the records into the case, snapped the lid shut, and carried the phonograph to his couch. There, pausing often to stare at the canvas and listen, he dug earth from the wall and disclosed a piece of board. Behind this there was a deep hole in the wall, into which he put the phonograph. After a moment's consideration he went over and reached down his bundle of books and inserted it also. Then, gradually, he once more sealed up the hole with the board and the earth. He also changed his blankets and the grass-stuffed sack which served as a pillow, so that he could lie facing the entrance. After carefully placing two more blocks of peat upon the fire he stood for a long time watching the stretched canvas, but it seemed to billow naturally with the first gusts of a lowering wind. At last he prayed, and got in under his blankets, and closed his smoke-smarting eyes. On the inside of the bed, next the wall, he could feel with his hand, the comfortable piece of lead pipe.

Was the professor overreacting? Would the other men rush his dugout and steal his cultural treasures? Does the "comfortable" lead pipe symbolize, say, an abundance of missiles poised in hardened silos? The story can be read on several levels, but it may suggest that the relationship between war and the higher learning can be studied on the human as well as the institutional scale.

Note-taking

Some students take notes on cards, some on ordinary sheets of paper. Students who take notes on cards are often very neat and orderly. They like to flash a thick deck of cards around, or, worse, carry their cards in a sturdy green tin box with a lid that snaps. Taking notes on cards does have at least one advantage, however. It allows you to shuffle specific ideas and information so you can write your paper. If you prefer to take notes on paper rather than on cards, plan to begin a fresh sheet for each separate idea or each set of data to make it easier to organize your findings.

Bibliography cards Before taking any notes on a particular source, you want to get down all pertinent bibliographic information about the source. Some instructors prefer you enter this information on separate cards, one source per card. You will need this information later on during the writing of the paper to document your sources. Your bibliography cards should contain the following information:

For books: author(s), title, city of publication, publisher, year of publication.

For an essay, poem, or story in a book of works by different writers: author(s), title of essay, poem, or story, title of book, editor(s) of book, city of publication, publisher, year of publication, and inclusive page numbers of the essay, poem, or story.

For reference works: author (s) or contributor(s) (if known), title of entry (if any), title of reference work, year of publication or number of edition, volume number (if any), inclusive page numbers of entry.

For magazine articles: author(s), title of article, name of magazine, volume number, date of publication, and inclusive page numbers of article.

For newspaper stories: reporter(s) or columnist(s) (if known), headline or title, name of newspaper, date of issue, number or letter of section, inclusive page numbers of story.

For interviews: name of person, occupation, official title or position (if any), organization (if any), and date of interview.

Sample bibliography cards appear below.

Note cards   You can take notes in several ways:

1.   Copy what you read word for word (direct quotation);
2.   Summarize what you read in your own words;
3.   Combine word-for-word copying and summarizing;
4.   Jot down crucial facts and statistics in shorthand, non-sentence notation;
5.   Respond to what you read or suggest how notes you take might be used later in your paper;
6.   Make copies of longer passages on copying machines and follow up with marginal notes.

arthur knight. *The Liveliest Art*, new york, mentor Books, 1957.

Ivan Illich. "Schooling: The
Ritual of Progress," New York
Review, XV, December 3, 1970,
p. 20-26.

David Hapgood. "The Diploma:
a meaningless, if Powerful,
Piece of Paper," Los Angeles
Times, August 3, 1969,
sec. F, p. 1-2.

Generally, you'll want to copy word for word only the most pertinent, most crucial, and best written passages you read. The passages
you copy should express thoughts that go to the heart of your research question and are so well put you couldn't begin to match
them in your own words. Passages you copy should also, perhaps,
be written by persons who are notable in some way: They are
recognized experts, they are directly involved in issues, they sum
up arguments or make eloquent pleas. *Make sure you enclose whatever you copy word for word in quotation marks.*

Summarize less crucial passages, perhaps those that are more factual or explanatory or that do not lend themselves to word-for-word quotation. Read a passage you intend to summarize carefully and make sure your summary does not distort the writer's ideas. Try to pick up all the main ideas of the passage in the same order and proportion. Condense and combine lesser ideas to form larger ideas you can write down in a sentence or two. Also, make sure your summary *is in your own words.* If you must use the words of the writer because you can think of none better, put quotation marks around them. One good way to avoid confusing the writer's wording and phrasing with your own is to summarize the passage *without looking at it.*

Below is a passage of explanation and opinion followed by several note cards. The note cards are headed by the author's last name and the page number of the passage on which notes were taken. Some note cards contain summaries, some quotations.

THE TYRANNY OF SOUND

In 1929, after little more than a year of talkies, *Variety* wryly reported, "Sound didn't do any more to the industry than turn it upside down, shake the entire bag of tricks from its pocket and advance Warner Brothers from the last place [among the film companies] to first in the league." The films had learned to talk, and talk was uppermost in everyone's mind. Script writers who had trained themselves to think in terms of pictures gave way to playwrights who thought in terms of stage dialogue. Established directors were either replaced by directors from the New York stage or supplemented by special dialogue directors. Many a popular star—especially the European importees—suddenly found himself unemployed; while the Broadway stage was again swept clean to replace those actors whose foreign accents, faulty diction or bad voices the temperamental microphone rejected. To fill the need for dialogue at all costs, plays—good, bad and indifferent—were bought up and rushed before the cameras. It was the era satirized in George S. Kaufman's *Once in a Lifetime,* when the Mr. Glo-gauers of Hollywood were valiantly but vainly trying to understand the change that had come over their industry, when self-styled geniuses were able to make incredible blunders simply because no one else had any better idea of how the talkies should be made.

And then a new and imposing figure appeared in the studios, the sound expert. It was the sound expert who concealed the microphone in the vase of flowers on the boudoir table, who dictated where actors must stand in order to record properly, who decided where the camera must be placed in order to keep the microphone outside its field. He was the final arbiter on what could and what could not be done, and his word was law. The camera itself, now imprisoned within a sound-proof booth, was robbed of all mobility. And the experts, concerned with nothing beyond the sound quality of the pictures they worked on, continually simplified their problems by insisting that scenes be played in corners, minimizing long-shots for the more readily controllable close-up. In no time at all the techniques, the artistry that directors had acquired through years of silent films were cast aside and forgotten in the shadow of the microphone.

Summary

Knight, p. 147 - "The Tyranny of Sound"
The advent of sound caused
much confusion. Script writers
for silent films were out of
work. So were the old directors.
The demand was for writers
and directors with stage
experience.

Summary and quotation

Knight, p. 148 - Enter a new
figure: the sound expert,
who decided where actors
and cameras should be
placed. "He was the final
arbiter on what could and
what could not be done, and
his word was law."

> Knight, p. 148.
>
> "The camera itself, now imprisoned within a sound-proof booth, was robbed of all mobility."

> Knight, p. 148.
>
> "In no time at all the techniques, the artistry that directors had acquired through the years of silent films were cast aside and forgotten in the shadow of the microphone."

Here is a passage of opinion, followed by several note cards:

The American university has become the final stage of the most all-encompassing initiation rite the world has ever known. No society in history has been able to survive without ritual or myth, but ours is the first which has needed such a dull, protracted, destructive, and expensive initiation into its myth. We cannot begin a reform of education unless we first understand that neither individual learning nor social equality can be enhanced by the ritual of schooling. We cannot go beyond the consumer society unless we first understand that obligatory public schools inevitably reproduce such a society, no matter what is taught in them.

The project of de-mythologizing which I propose cannot be limited to the university alone. Any attempt to reform the university without attending to the system of which it is an integral part is like trying to do urban renewal in New York City from the twelfth story up. Most current college level reform looks like the building of high-rise slums. Only a generation which grows up without obligatory schools will be able to re-create the university.

Summary and quotation

Illich, p. 21 — Illich feels that college is an "initiation rite" unmatched by any society because it is so "dull, protracted, destructive, and expensive..." "the ritual of schooling" has little to do with "individual learning" or "social equality."

Summary and response

Illich, p. 21 — To improve on the "consumer society" we must first reform our schools, because schools produce consumers, regardless of what they actually teach. (Relate this to the defense economy.)

> *Illich, p 21. — Illich claims the universities cannot be reformed until the schools are reformed. "Only a gener- ation which grows up with- out obligatory schools will be able to re-create the univ- ersity." (Wow! Big job. Is he asking too much?)*

Here is another passage, primarily factual, followed by a single note card:

Education now spends $58 billion a year, second only to the military and coming up fast. (Some defense contractors such as Raytheon and Litton have been buying into the school business as a hedge against the danger of peace.)

Measured in time, the power of education is still more impressive. More than 60 million Americans are engaged full time in the industry—57 mil- lion as students, 3 million as teachers and administrators. It may well be that the time devoted to school is growing faster than our life expectancy.

Nonsentence notation

> *Hapgood, p. F-1*
> *— Education: $58 billion a year*
> *— second to military*
> *— 60 million full-time*
> *(57 million students, 3 million teachers + administration)*
> *These figures for 1970 —*

be valuable even economically, whereas accumulating Regents blue-books is worth nothing except to the school itself.

(By and large, it is not in the adolescent years but in later years that, in all walks of life, there is need for academic withdrawal, periods of study and reflection, synoptic review of the texts. The Greeks understood this and regarded most of our present college curricula as appropriate for only those over the age of thirty or thirty-five. To some extent, the churches used to provide a studious environment. We do these things miserably in hurried conferences.)

We have similar problems in the universities. We cram the young with what they do not want at the time and what most of them will never use; but by requiring graded diplomas we make it hard for older people to get what they want and can use. Now, paradoxically, when so many are going to school, the training of authentic learned professionals is proving to be a failure, with dire effects on our ecology, urbanism, polity, communications, and even the direction of science. Doing others' lessons under compulsion for twenty years does not tend to produce professionals who are autonomous, principled, and ethically responsible to client and community. Broken by processing, professionals degenerate to mere professional-personnel. Professional peer groups have become economic lobbies. The licensing and maintenance of standards have been increasingly relinquished to the state, which has no competence.

In licensing professionals, we have to look more realistically at functions, drop mandarin requirements of academic diplomas that are irrelevant, and rid ourselves of the ridiculous fad of awarding diplomas for every skill and trade whatever. In most professions and arts there are important abstract parts that can best be learned academically. The natural procedure is for those actually engaged in a professional activity to go to school to learn what they now know they need; re-entry into the academic track, therefore, should be made easy for those with a strong motive.

Universities are primarily schools of learned professions, and the faculty should be composed primarily not of academics but of working professionals who feel duty-bound and attracted to pass on their tradition to apprentices of a new generation. Being combined in a community of scholars, such professionals teach a noble apprenticeship, humane and with vision toward a more ideal future. It is humane because the disciplines communicate with one another; it is ideal because the young are free and questioning. A good professional school can be tiny. In *The Community of Scholars* I suggest that 150 students and ten professionals—the size of the usual medieval university—are

enough. At current faculty salaries, the cost per student would be a fourth of that of our huge administrative machines. And, of course, on such a small scale contact between faculty and students is sought for and easy.

Today, because of the proved incompetence of our adult institutions and the hypocrisy of most professionals, university students have a right to a large say in what goes on. (But this, too, is medieval.) Professors will, of course, teach what they please. My advice to students is that given by Prince Kropotkin, in "A Letter to the Young": "Ask what kind of world do you want to live in? What are you good at and want to work at to build that world? What do you need to know? Demand that your teachers teach you that." Serious teachers would be delighted by this approach.

The idea of the liberal arts college is a beautiful one: to teach the common culture and refine character and citizenship. But it does not happen; the evidence is that the college curriculum has little effect on underlying attitudes, and most cultivated folk do not become so by this route. School friendships and the community of youth do have lasting effects, but these do not require ivied clubhouses. Young men learn more about the theory and practice of government by resisting the draft than they ever learned in Political Science 412.

MUCH of the present university expansion, needless to say, consists in federal-and corporation-contracted research and other research and has nothing to do with teaching. Surely such expansion can be better carried on in the Government's and corporations' own institutes, which would be unencumbered by the young, except those who are hired or attach themselves as apprentices.

Every part of education can be open to need, desire, choice, and trying out. Nothing needs to be compelled or extrinsically motivated by prizes and threats. I do not know if the procedure here outlined would cost more than our present system—though it is hard to conceive of a need for more money than the school establishment now spends. What would be saved is the pitiful waste of youthful years—caged, daydreaming, sabotaging, and cheating—and the degrading and insulting misuse of teachers.

It has been estimated by James Coleman that the average youth in high school is really "there" about ten minutes a day. Since the growing-up of the young into society to be useful to themselves and others, and to do God's work, is one of the three or four most important functions of any society, no doubt we ought to spend even more on the education of the young than we do; but I would not give a penny to the present administrators, and I would largely dismantle the present school machinery.

Relate to Illich

Quote this

Look into this book?

Relate to Ridgeway and Military-Industrial complex

More waste

Using copying machines Copying machines are very useful for page-long or multiple-page passages of materials you want to use. The copying machine in your library will probably cost you at least a dime per copy page, and the cost can run up fast. You can save money by making sure you don't make copies of materials you don't need. Read over the chapter or the article you plan to machine copy and at least think through a summary before changing down your last dollar to dimes. You might find you can do without certain pages.

You can make various notes on the pages of materials you have copied from machines. Draw boxes around crucial paragraphs. Underline key sentences, facts, and statistics. Make marginal notes to remind you of the importance of various passages. Sample annotated page from a machine-copied article appears on page 63.

AFTERCHAPTER
___

The Longer Paper

Begin reading to answer your research question. Spend a few days reading general background material to get the feel of your specific topic before settling down to answer your research question. Take notes on pertinent facts, statistics, examples, commentary, and so forth. Fill out bibliography cards accurately and completely.
___

Activities

1. Read the selection below. Take notes on it, as follows:
    A. Isolate five key facts or statistics.
    B. Copy down five key sentences word for word. Make sure the sentences are notable and quotable.
    C. Select two paragraphs to summarize *in fewer words, in your own words.*

TOO LITTLE FOOD

Why did I pick on the next nine years instead of the next 900 for finding a solution to the population crisis? One answer is that the world, especially the undeveloped world, is rapidly running out of food. And famine, of course, could be one way to reach a death rate solution to the population problem. In fact, the battle to feed humanity is already lost, in the sense that we will not be able to prevent large-scale famines in the next decade or so. It is difficult to guess what the exact scale and consequences of the famines will be. But there *will be* famines. Let's look at the situation today.

Everyone agrees that at least half of the people of the world are undernourished (have too little food) or malnourished (have serious imbalances in their diet). The number of deaths attributable to starvation is open to considerable debate. The reason is threefold. First, demographic statistics are often incomplete or unreliable. Second, starving people don't necessarily die of starvation. They often fall victim to some disease as they weaken. When good medical care is available, starvation can be a long, drawn-out process indeed. Third, and perhaps more important, starvation is undramatic. Deaths from starvation go unnoticed, even when they occur as close as Mississippi. Many Americans are under the delusion that an Asian can live happily "on a bowl of rice a day." Such a diet means slow starvation for an Asian, just as it would for an American. A *New Republic* article estimated that five million Indian children die each year of malnutrition. The Population Crisis Committee estimates that three and one-half million people will starve to death this year, mostly children. Senator George McGovern called hunger "the chief killer of man."

Through the first decade following World War II, food production per person in the UDCs kept up with population growth. Then, sometime around 1958, "the stork passed the plow." Serious transfers of food began from the DCs to the UDCs. As food got scarcer, economic laws of supply and demand began to take effect in the UDCs. Food prices began to rise. Marginal land began to be brought into production—as evidenced by reduced yields per acre. In short, all the signs of an approaching food crisis began to appear. Then in 1965–1966 came the first dramatic blow.

In 1965–1966 mankind suffered a shocking defeat in what is now popularly called the "war on hunger." In 1966, while the population of the world increased by some 70 million people, there was *no* compensatory increase in food production. According to the United Nations Food and Agriculture Organization (FAO), advances in food production made in developing nations between 1955 and 1965 were wiped out by agricultural disasters in 1965 and 1966. In 1966 each person on Earth had 2% less to eat, the reduction, of course, not being uniformly distributed. Only ten countries grew more food than they consumed: the United States, Canada, Australia, Argentina, France, New Zealand, Burma, Thailand, Rumania, and South Africa. The United States produced more than half of the surplus, with Canada and Australia contributing most of the balance. All other countries, including the giants of China, India, and Russia, imported more than they exported. In 1966 the United States shipped *one quarter* of its wheat crop, nine million tons, to India. In the process we helped change the distribution of people in the country. Thousands migrated into port cities so as to be close to the centers of wheat distribution. We also, in the opinion of some, hindered India's own agricultural development. Perhaps we gave too many Indians the impression that we have an unlimited capacity to ship them food. Unhappily, we do not.

In 1967 we were extremely fortunate in having a fine growing year almost worldwide. If the predicted harvests actually materialize (we will not know until some months after this is written), the amount of food produced per person will be 5 or 6% above the 1966 levels. But it will still not be up to the 1964 level. This partial recovery, due largely to good weather, seems to have shifted some agriculturists (especially in the U.S. Department of Agriculture) from pessimism to limited optimism about the world food situation. True, there are hopeful signs especially in the form of new wheat and rice varieties. But we're not even in a position to evaluate the true potential of these developments, let alone assign to them the panacea role so devoutly wished for by many.

Nowhere is hoping more of a habit than in the Indian government. Madan G. Kaul, Minister of the Indian Embassy, addressing the Second International Conference on the War on Hunger, hoped that his country would be self-sufficient in food by 1971. If only hoping would make it so! To put this fantasy into perspective, you must know that this means the

Indians hope to be able to feed 50 to 70 million more people in four years than they *cannot* feed today. Their population is growing at a rate of 14 to 18 million people per year.

2. Reread the selection "Too Little Food," above. Take whatever notes pertain to the following research questions:
   A. Can underdeveloped countries grow enough food in the future to feed their peoples?
   B. What has been the effect of "have" nations, like the U.S., exporting surplus food to "have not" nations?

3. Below are some suggested mini-research projects. First, match a topic with a project. Examples:
   1. Research the history of Christmas.
   2. Find out what the experts have said about raising gifted children.

Topics	*Research Projects*
A. A sport.	1. Investigate the history of the topic.
B. A hobby.	
C. Pollution.	2. Identify pros and cons.
D. A holiday.	3. Determine important facts or statistics.
E. Child raising.	
F. Crime.	4. Read experts on the topic and respond to their views.
G. City planning.	
H. Abortion.	5. Read about several related topics and formulate general principles.
I. Violence.	
J. Television.	
K. A topic of your choice.	

Now find at least two sources bearing on your topic-project. Read pertinent passages in these sources and take notes. Write a short paper about your findings.

6

Posing a Thesis and Refining It

When do you finally answer your research question? How much do you have to read first? That depends. Some students glimpse the answers to their research questions after looking into only a book or two. But usually they keep reading anyway, to test their first hunches and sharpen their conclusions. Other students hold off on answering their research questions until they think all the returns are in, or until a deadline looms and forces them to break off their readings. There are students who perceive the answers to their research questions in a moment of sudden insight—*click!*—and there are students for whom answers emerge slowly and laboriously —*whir, whir*. . . .

At any rate, there comes a time during your research when you have to cease your readings and start thinking about writing your paper. When you feel you have the answer to the question you asked, when you feel informed and confident, you can start putting your findings together to plan your paper. You have learned a lot from your readings, but chances are your findings are somewhat jumbled and disconnected like the parts of a clock spread out before you. How do you put it all together to write a paper?

You first pose a *thesis*. A thesis is more than just an answer to a research question. It is a brief statement you write that serves as a halfway point of research. Looking back, a thesis combines and relates your most important or most interesting conclusions. Looking ahead, a thesis provides a framework for writing your paper. Posing a thesis helps you connect reading and writing. If you fail to pose a thesis, you may not be able to form unified conclusions about your research topic; without uniform conclusions your finished paper might read like an assorted list of findings without relatedness, direction, or purpose. Posing a thesis, therefore, is a very important step toward the completion of your paper.

Sample theses:

The advent of sound in 1927 at first posed a threat to the developing art of cinema, and only gradually won a place in the repertoire of editing principles established during the silent era.

Like other overgrown institutions, our college system has become self-serving and wasteful, and its influence should now be restricted to allow alternatives to flourish.

There are advantages in posing a thesis as a single sentence. A sentence restricts and relates thought. It forces decisions about what is or is not important. It is also a whole, complete statement whose part-ideas are connected by the sentence's structure. A paper, too, is a whole statement made up of connected part-ideas. The wholeness of the thesis sentence is a sort of seed out of which the wholeness of the paper grows. You may, of course, use several sentences to write your thesis; but you run the risk of dealing with too many ideas, and the resulting paper may lack the restriction and relatedness you want to communicate clearly.

Posing the thesis

A thesis is usually arrived at after studying notes and looking for findings that can be grouped together. These grouped findings, or conclusions, are in turn related, refined, and combined into a single, brief, unifying statement. This statement is the thesis, the framework for the finished paper. To illustrate the process:

Research question: What impact did the advent of sound in 1927 have on the later development of film art?

Conclusions based on notes:

1. D. W. Griffith and Sergei Eisenstein pioneered the art of film editing during the silent film era.
2. Attendance at movies began to slump in the late twenties.
3. Lee De Forest and the German firm Tri-Ergon developed the optical sound system promoted by movie executive William Fox.
4. Movie attendance doubled after the advent of sound in 1927.
5. The earliest sound films used sound clumsily and excessively.
6. At first sound threatened to cancel the achievements of filmmakers such as Griffith and Eisenstein because it distracted from the visual art.
7. Color was introduced not long after sound.
8. Wide-screen formats were introduced in the fifties to meet the challenge of TV.
9. Filmmakers of the thirties learned to use sound to extend the editing principles of the silent era: Not only

picture-to-picture, but sound-to-picture and sound-to-sound relationships were explored.

What sense can be made of these conclusions? Some refinements are first in order. If the researcher is more interested in the effects of sound than in how sound came to be introduced, he might deemphasize conclusions 2, 3, and 4 by grouping them:

The optical sound system was introduced by businessmen to increase attendance at movies.

Conclusions 7 and 8, about color and wide screen, seem off the main line of inquiry and probably should be cut. A refined list of conclusions might read:

1. D. W. Griffith and Sergei Eisenstein pioneered the art of film editing during the silent film era.
2. The optical sound system was introduced by businessmen in 1928 to increase attendance at movies.
3. The earliest sound films used sound clumsily and excessively.
4. At first sound threatened to cancel the achievements of filmmakers such as Griffith and Eisenstein because it distracted from the visual factor.
5. Filmmakers of the thirties learned to use sound to extend the editing principles of the silent era: Not only picture-to-picture, but sound-to-picture and sound-to-sound relationships were explored.

Now the conclusions are tighter and better related. A thesis can be written:

The advent of sound in 1927 at first posed a threat to the developing art of cinema, and only gradually won a place in the repertoire of editing principles established during the silent era.

A second illustration of the same process:

Research question: What is the connection between the so-called military-industrial complex and our system of college education?

Conclusions based on notes:

1. Large institutions often become very inefficient and self-serving.
2. The expansionist military-industrial complex led us into Vietnam at a great cost of lives, money, and resources.
3. Many of our leading universities are deeply involved in war-related research—often at the expense of students.
4. Many politicians now advocate abolishing the draft.
5. There are so many loopholes in the present draft laws

that nearly any persevering young man can "buy out" with the aid of a good lawyer.

6. Colleges have been growing, and education as a whole is America's second biggest industry after defense.
7. Studies show a poor relationship between performance in college and later performance on the job.
8. If the colleges were scaled down, viable alternatives for learning might flourish.

These conclusions, obviously, are more far-ranging than the first set of conclusions about motion pictures; they touch on Vietnam, the draft, jobs, colleges, and alternatives to colleges. It is not likely that any single statement can unify all of them. But nearly all the conclusions seem to relate to the first one, about how overgrown institutions are inefficient and wasteful. Conclusion 2 applies this principle to the military. Conclusion 3 links the military and the colleges and suggests more self-serving. Conclusions 6 and 7 together imply waste and inefficiency as a result of growth. And conclusion 8 suggests the converse of conclusions 6 and 7, that is, a scaled-down system of college education might prove more responsive. But conclusions 4 and 5, about the draft, do not contribute much to this progression of ideas. If conclusions 4 and 5 were dropped, the following thesis might unify the remaining six conclusions:

> Like other overgrown institutions, our college system has become self-serving and wasteful, and its influence should now be restricted to allow alternatives to flourish.

As this thesis is written, it is clear that the researcher intends to stress the reform of colleges in his paper, though he apparently will also refer to other large institutions in order to develop his ideas.

Refining the thesis

But probably your thesis will require some polishing and refining before it can serve as a guide for writing your paper. To refine your thesis, you may have to reread your notes and draw new conclusions. But if your thesis still doesn't sound right to you, this could mean you still have gaps in your research, and you may have to do some more reading. Below is a list of problems that commonly afflict first theses, along with suggestions for follow-up reading:

The thesis is too broad, vague, or incomplete
First theses:
1. There are many causes of violence.
2. The future of architecture is very challenging.
3. The family unit should be strengthened.

Critique. All of these theses have a similar problem: They fail to focus on specific aspects of the topics they treat, and lacking focus they are vague or incomplete in thought. Papers based on them could also lack focus and come off vague and incomplete. Would a paper based on thesis 1 discuss all types of violence? Would it merely itemize causes or would it deal with only key causes? What does "challenging" mean in thesis 2? Would the paper stress design, engineering, materials, environment, or what? What is meant by "strengthened" in thesis 3? Why does the "family unit" have to be strengthened? What threatens the family unit? Is "strengthened" the right word?

Additional readings. Some of these questions might be answered after restudying existing notes to get clear on the specific intent of the thesis. But a broad, vague, or seemingly incomplete thesis could mean spotty research. Follow-up readings might stress, for instance, a specific set of causes for a specific type of violence, say street crime. Or perhaps the researcher needs to read further about one aspect of the future of architecture, such as its role in urban renewal. Or perhaps more reading is necessary to clarify how family ties have been weakened.

Revised theses:

1. The nation's antiquated court system is a major cause of street crime.
2. As Americans turn their efforts toward making cities more liveable, architects will begin to explore new ways to develop low-cost, mass-produced housing.
3. Relationships among members of families could be improved if the family assumed a larger role in the nonacademic education of children.

The thesis advances too many ideas

First theses:

1. Street crime seems to be related to economic problems, but most murders are crimes of passion, while the causes of war are very complex.
2. In the future architects will develop new materials, experiment with new designs, study the behavioral sciences, and become involved with the human problems of urban renewal.
3. The automobile, in liberating youth, has been a principal cause of the deterioration of the family unit, while other institutions such as schools, hospitals, and nursing homes have also tended to pull the family apart.

Critique. These theses attempt too much. They need to be

pruned down, unless the students who wrote them intended to produce very long papers.

Additional readings. Paring down a thesis that advances too many ideas may require additional reading if previous research sacrificed depth for breadth. If a student decides he wants to write a paper about crimes of passion, he may want to read about the legal implications of such crimes; a student looking into the relationship of the behavioral sciences to architecture may want to read further about what living space has to do with compatibility; and the student who thinks cars have something to do with the generation gap might need to read some more about these two topics.

Revised theses:
1. Since most murders are crimes of passion, the death penalty has little deterrent effect on the homicide rate.
2. In the future architects will design dwellings to satisfy two basic and opposing human needs: privacy and companionship.
3. The automobile has had the effect of weakening family ties by giving youth a physical means of widening the generation gap.

The ideas of the thesis are poorly related
First theses:
1. Women are less physically aggressive than men, and the U.S. has had only male presidents, just as we have not backed down from wars.
2. Architects usually are employed to design private dwellings or office buildings, but in the future the nation will need millions of government-subsidized, low-cost family dwellings.
3. Schools now teach many nonacademic subjects, and the family has less of an influence on children.

Critique. These theses are not very easy to read, but they are not necessarily too broad, nor do they advance too many ideas. Rather the ideas each advances are not well related. And if the ideas of the theses are not connected well, the papers they generate could also be hard to follow.

Additional readings. A thesis with poorly related ideas might be rewritten and improved after the student goes over his notes again and rethinks the relationships among the ideas he intends to write about. But unclear relationships could mean incomplete research. Additional readings might be necessary to clarify relationships. Thesis 1, for instance, might be improved if the student read some more about the male and female egos. Thesis 2 seems to lack the suggestion that the role of the architect may shift in the future; would additional readings confirm this hunch? Thesis 3 isn't clear about what nonacademic subjects have to do with the family's waning influence; again, follow-up reading could clarify this relationship.

Revised theses:
1. Since women are less physically aggressive than men, a female president may be less inclined to involve the nation in war than a male president.
2. As the nation's priorities change, many architects will turn from designing private dwellings to designing low-cost public housing.
3. The schools, in assuming many of the educational functions the family once provided, have been a principal cause of the weakening of family ties.

The position the thesis takes is trite, obvious, too well known

First theses:
1. We should make an all-out effort to reduce street crime.
2. Architects play an important role in making the environment more liveable.
3. Parents and teenagers often fail to communicate with each other.

Critique. None of these theses tell readers anything they didn't already know. A trite thesis usually means an unpromising paper, unless the student has taken notes on more compelling aspects of his topic. If he has, the thesis should reflect this. Often, however, a trite thesis develops from a trite research question. The student reads and takes notes to confirm his prior sentiments, rather than to test them, and the entire research project ends up a sort of sterile exercise rather than the meaningful confrontation with new ideas it should be.

Additional readings. But trite theses don't have to be junked altogether. Usually, stale statements suggest all sorts of interesting questions: *that* we should reduce street crime is obvious enough, but *what* can be done is not so obvious. *How* do architects make the environment more liveable, and with whom do they work to improve the environment? What does "fail to communicate" really mean? Additional readings along these lines might yield enough *new* information to lead to more original and interesting theses.

Revised theses:
1. An all-out attack on poverty would significantly reduce street crime.
2. Architects work with social scientists to design dwell-

ings that reflect the living patterns and customs of certain ethnic groups.
3. Lack of mutual respect is the principal cause of the
so-called generation gap.

Further refinements

But even when your thesis finally reads well, it may not square
with your conscience. You may want to tinker with it a bit more to
make sure it sets up the kind of paper you really want to write. Here
are three further areas of refinement that even well-phrased theses
may require.

Certain ideas are incompletely researched

Revised thesis: In the future architects will design dwellings to satisfy two basic and opposing human needs: privacy
and companionship.

Suppose the student is certain he wants to write his paper from
this thesis, but he feels his research in the area of designing dwellings for privacy is sketchy. He had gathered enough material to
write with confidence about what architects have done to promote
companionship, but he thinks he had better gather more information and examples about designing to promote privacy. Additional
readings to support this aspect of the thesis may be required before
the student feels ready to write his paper.

The thesis misses a basic point

Revised thesis: Since most murders are crimes of passion,
the death penalty has little deterrent effect on the homicide
rate.

No matter how well the student can support this thesis with his
research notes, he may decide the thesis is not quite right. It is not
the vision he had, not the answer he sought, not what he really had
in mind. The thesis may miss a basic point the student felt he
wanted to work with but, for whatever reason, did not. Suppose, for
instance, the student decides he really hadn't intended to explore
the nature of murder or the deterrent value of the death penalty;
instead he really wants to explore why Americans still tolerate the
death penalty in the face of evidence that it doesn't reduce crime.

To explore this point, however, the student may have to reopen
his research. Suppose, after further readings, he posed this thesis:

Final revision: Americans tolerate the death penalty because they have a vindictive rather than a corrective attitude toward crime.

Whether you should reopen your research to explore a new point
that you want to make depends on how much time you have and

how strongly you feel about the point. If the deadline for the finished paper is drawing near, you may have to go ahead and write your paper based on your original thesis, even if the thesis doesn't really reflect your true interests. But before you do, see your teacher and explain the situation to him; he may agree to extend the deadline for your finished paper.

The position the thesis takes may need to be modified

Revised thesis: The schools, in assuming many of the educational functions the family once provided, have been a principal cause of the weakening of family ties.

Nearly any thesis that has a persuasive edge to it, such as the one above, should probably be tested by additional reading. The student may want to change his mind. Further readings may reveal that the position of the first thesis was in need of modification: The position may have been oversimplified, or misinformed, or perhaps even unreasonable. On the other hand, additional reading may reveal that the researcher's first instincts were essentially sound. He may not care to change his stand at all; instead he may, after further reading, grow even more secure in his convictions. The point is, you should regard your first thesis as just a hunch, and as such requiring some follow-up reading to prove its worth. Suppose, for instance, the student suspects that he may have oversimplified the relationship between the expanding role of the school and the weakening ties of families. Additional reading into the causes of the so-called breakdown of the family might turn up a few new ideas to be fed into the thesis:

Final revision: The expanding educational roles of schools have contributed to a weakening of family ties, but the changing nature of the family is also a function of deeper social and cultural changes that work on both schools and families.

Strategies for follow-up readings

Often the process of refining a thesis after additional readings requires what amounts to the formulation of one or more new research questions. These new questions are usually related to the original question, but they may suggest different strategies for following-up reading. Example:

Original question: What is the connection between the so-called military-industrial complex and our system of college education? (Strategy: relation)

First thesis: Both the military and colleges have become wasteful.

Critique of first thesis: Vague and incomplete; ideas poorly related; may miss a basic point: what can be done to reduce waste?

Question for follow-up reading: What deficiencies of large institutions in general may apply to the nation's college system? (Strategy: comparison or deduction)

Additional question for follow-up reading: What alternatives to college for learning and job training have been proposed? (Strategy: itemization)

Revised thesis: Like other overgrown institutions, our college system has become self-serving and wasteful, and its influence should now be restricted to allow alternatives to flourish.

Thus a research project that began in readings intended to relate two institutions led the researcher first to compare institutions and form general principles about them, and second to seek solutions for the problems implied by the general principles. The thesis suggests that the completed paper will first explain problems (colleges, like other institutions, have in some ways become wasteful and self-serving) and then advance solutions (a number of alternatives to college).

Not all research projects need to shift strategies this way. Often the same strategy implied by the original question is pursued through to the refined thesis and the finished paper. Shifting strategies can be confusing and time-consuming. Whether or not you should pursue new strategies and pose new questions depends almost entirely on you, and what you most want to learn, what you most want to write about later. But this much can be said in favor of pursuing additional strategies: it allows you to approach your chosen topic from several useful perspectives so that, in the end, you could be better informed about it.

AFTERCHAPTER

The Longer Paper

Pose a thesis based on your notes and revise it to make it say what you want it to say and to serve as a framework for writing your paper. If necessary, complete additional readings before attempting to refine the thesis.

Activities

1. Study the following lists of conclusions and pose a thesis for each set. Example:
    Conclusions based on notes:
    A. Overpopulation leads to starvation, wars, rioting, and excessive pollution.

B. The world's population will double by the year 2000.
C. Moslem religious tenets obstruct birth control programs in such overpopulated countries as Indonesia and Pakistan.
D. In overpopulated South America, the Catholic Church opposes birth control measures.

Possible theses:

The problems of overpopulation will not be solved until the world's major religions modify their positions on birth control.

The world's major religions stand in the way of proposals to control population and alleviate the problems of overpopulation.

Conclusions based on notes:

A. Stutterers usually have no physical impairments of the organs of speech.
B. Feelings of insecurity and inadequacy usually accompany stuttering.
C. Some stutterers display mixed dominance of the hemispheres of the brain. (The left side of the brain doesn't control the right side of the body, or vice versa, as it should.)
D. The majority of stutterers, however, display normal hemispheric dominance.
E. Speech therapists have had little success correcting stuttering by means of speech exercises intended to affect the muscles of the organs of speech.
F. As the stutterer improves his outlook on life, his speech usually improves too.

Conclusions based on notes:

A. Eighty percent of exconvicts are convicted of crimes again and returned to prison.
B. Former Attorney-General Ramsey Clark feels that prisons manufacture crime: Less experienced inmates learn techniques of crime from older inmates.
C. Homosexuality is common in our prisons.
D. Most prison wardens and their staffs lack training in the behavioral sciences.
E. History offers almost no examples of societies achieving significant reductions in crime by keeping criminals in prisons.

2. All of the following first theses need revision. Which (a) are too broad, vague, or seemingly incomplete, (b) advance too many ideas, (c) fail to relate their ideas well, (d) are too trite or obvious? Which theses have more than one problem?

A. While religious views are related to personality, some young people are responding to a new image of Jesus as a sort of social reformer who fights poverty, racism, and war.
B. Divorce causes many problems.
C. Automobile manufacturers want to maximize profits while a new breed of automotive engineers stresses safety.
D. Birth control pills can help parents limit the size of their families, but the Catholic Church is opposed to birth control pills, and some medical researchers have found that prolonged use of birth control pills could have adverse side effects.
E. Smoking is harmful to your health.

F. Astrology explains personality in a way that appeals to certain people.
G. The well-adjusted person sets goals for himself, is happy, realistic, practical, and knows his own limitations, but he never gives up either.
H. Although John Muir was mostly self-educated, he led the fight to establish a system of national parks.
I. The government has the right to protect people from their own ignorance, and the laws regulating drug use are no different.
J. The communes of Israel are different from the communes of the United States.

3. Select any *four* topics listed below and work each into a separate thesis sentence. Critique your theses and rewrite them if necessary. Base your theses on your own opinions, experiences, or present knowledge.
Topics:
A. The perfect classroom.
B. What's wrong (or right) about TV.
C. Drugs.
D. Love.
E. The ideal job.
F. Your hero.
G. A movie you can't get out of your head.
H. Birth control information for college students.
I. Our programmed society.
J. Why you hate your (father, mother, studies, job, car, girlfriend, boyfriends, self, or ?).
K. Doing your own thing. (Specify: what thing?)
L. Not being able to do your own thing. (Specify.)
M. Other people's things. (Specify.)
N. Things
O. Anything (a topic of your choice).

4. Select any thesis you wrote and refined for activity 3. Write a short paper based on the thesis.

III
WRITING

The self-educated are marked by stubborn peculiarities.

—Isaac D'Israeli

Self-education is fine when the pupil is a born educator.

—John A. Shedd

7
Outlining the Paper

The Great Outline War usually shapes up like this: On one side are students, who either fear outlines or are bored by writing them. On the other side are teachers, who insist no student can produce a readable paper unless he first outlines his ideas. Some students maintain that it is a long jump from an outline to a finished paper, and a lot can happen to alter all those nice plans and neatly fitting As, Bs, and Cs. Outlining, these students point out, is rigid and fussy, while writing should be loose and free. Teachers, in turn, try to point out that effective writing is not exactly loose and free, and the research paper especially, if it is to succeed, must be tight and controlled. Teachers nearly always win this war.

This chapter attempts to negotiate a truce agreeable to both sides. On the one hand, you obviously should do some thinking before writing up the findings of your research. To produce a research paper of five or ten or more pages whose ideas hang together and point the reader in one direction, you must have some notion beforehand of what information you will present and in what order. But on the other hand, it is nearly impossible to outline every detail of your paper before you write it. You'll have to write your way into and out of these details. Thus, while you should develop some kind of outline to help you get started on your paper, you probably won't be able to write a detailed outline, nor should you want to.

"Some kind of outline" means a working outline. A working outline is brief and general. It is subject to change. It should, in fact, change as the writing of the paper itself produces new and better ideas, or reveals that the ideas of the outline are in need of refinement. A working outline allows you to get started on the writing of your paper. But it is suggestive rather than restrictive. It is like an embryo whose chromosomes determine a few broad features of the later mature individual, but the individual himself is his own creation, growing and becoming on his own.

The main purpose of any outline, working or otherwise, is to show relationships among ideas. General ideas in outlines serve as categories for more specific member-ideas; the member-ideas can also serve as categories for still more specific member-ideas, and on and on until one runs out of categories or members or patience. Many entries in an outline can be regarded as either categories or as members of a category. An entry is a category relative to the entries of the step below it; it is a member of a category relative to the entry of the step above it.

    I. Trees
        A. Softwood trees
           1. Pines
           2. Firs
        B. Hardwood trees
           1. Oaks
           2. Maples

Thus the entry "Softwood trees" serves as a *category* for the members "Pines" and "Firs" (a step below) while it is a *member* of the category "Trees" (a step above).

The teachers that taught you outlining probably insisted that if you entered an "A" you must also enter at least a "B"; if you have a "1" you must have at least a "2." This is because every category has at least two members, else it is not a category. Thus

        A. Softwood trees
           1. Pines
               a. Sugar pine
           2. Firs
               a. Douglas fir

is faulty because it makes a claim, in essence, that the category "Pines" has but one member and the category "Firs" has but one member. If no more than one member of a category comes to mind, then the category has to be junked since it isn't really a category. The single entry then is incorporated into the next entry a step above:

        A. Softwood trees
           1. Sugar pine
           2. Douglas fir

Outlines deal with categories and members of categories this way because the ideas of your paper will have a similar relationship. Some ideas of your paper will be more general than others. You should treat these general ideas as categories, and as such having at least two member-ideas. But each member-idea may often be regarded as a category too, each with its more specific member-ideas.

The terms *specific* and *general* therefore are relative in the same way the terms *member* and *category* are relative. An idea is specific relative to a more general idea it stems from, but it is general relative to more specific ideas it generates. The secret in achieving length—five, ten, twenty pages—in college writing (or any writing) lies in discovering a number of related general ideas to write about, and for each general idea establishing a number of specific ideas which in turn may produce still more specific ideas.

The outline in practice

If you arrived at your thesis in some way similar to the procedures described in the last chapter, you have already begun work on your outline. A thesis, as we have seen, is often arrived at by grouping individual notes, drawing conclusions, and combining these conclusions into a single, unified statement. An outline can be developed by reversing this procedure. Here are some steps you might follow for developing an outline:

1. *Study your refined thesis and isolate the main ideas it suggests.* Write these main ideas as separate, complete sentences:

> *Thesis:* The advent of sound in 1927 at first posed a threat to the developing art of cinema, and only gradually won a place in the repertoire of editing principles established during the silent era.
>
> *Main ideas:*
> I. At first sound threatened the developing art of cinema.
> II. Later on, sound won its place in the repertoire of editing principles.
> III. Principles of film editing were first established during the silent-film era.

2. *Next, determine a best order for these main idea sentences.* If your thesis embodies one of the common strategies of research discussed in previous chapters, the strategy itself might suggest a best order for the main ideas of your outline: cause *then* effect, problem *then* solution, general principle *then* specific application. In the example below, the strategies of time and cause and effect establish the order of the main ideas:

> I. Principles of film editing were first established during the silent-film era.
> II. At first sound threatened the developing art of cinema.
> III. Later on, sound won its place in the repertoire of editing principles.

3. *Now regard each main idea sentence as a category.* Sort through your notes to find pertinent quotations, facts, examples, and the like which are members of these main-idea categories. In

effect, "deal out" your notes in stacks, each stack corresponding to a main idea. Notes for main idea II:

II. At first sound inhibited the emerging art of cinema.

Notes:

1) Attendance at movies had declined by 1926.

2) The first talkie, "The Jazz Singer" with Al Jolsen, appeared in 1927, and by 1929 movie attendance had doubled.

3) Arthur Knight quotes *Variety:* " 'Sound didn't do any more to the industry than turn it upside down, shake the entire bag of tricks from its pocket and advance Warner Brothers from last place [among the film companies] to first in the league.' "

4) Arthur Knight: ". . . 1929 was for the most part the year of static, photographed stage plays, the year of the 'all-talking, all-singing' musical, the year which raw sound was exploited in every imaginable way."

5) Mack Sennett's *The Family Picnic* thrilled movie goers with the exaggerated sound of picnickers eating potato chips and celery.

6) Since cameras had to be housed in soundproof booths, scenes were shot from fixed ranges and angles, and takes were very long.

7) Ivor Montagu: "The resulting films were truly dull."

8) Knight: "In no time at all the techniques, the artistry that directors had acquired through the years of silent films were cast aside and forgotten in the shadow of the microphone."

4. *Now study the notes you assembled for each main idea.* Combine similar or related notes to establish intermediate categories for each main idea category:

II. At first sound inhibited the emerging art of cinema.

Category A:

1. Attendance at movies had declined by 1926.

2. The first talkie, *The Jazz Singer* with Al Jolsen, appeared in 1927, and by 1929 movie attendance had doubled.

3. Arthur Knight quotes *Variety:* " 'Sound didn't do any more to the industry than turn it upside down, shake the entire bag of tricks from its pocket and advance Warner Brothers from the last place [among the film companies] to first in the league.' "

Category B:

1. Arthur Knight: ". . . 1929 was for the most part the year

of static, photographed stage plays, the year of the 'all-talking, all-singing' musical, the year which raw sound was exploited in every imaginable way."

2. Mack Sennett's *The Family Picnic* thrilled movie goers with the exaggerated sound of picnickers eating potato chips and celery.

Category C:

1. Since cameras had to be housed in soundproof booths, scenes were shot from fixed ranges and angles, and takes were very long.

2. Ivor Montagu: "The resulting films were truly dull."

3. Knight: "In no time at all the techniques, the artistry that directors had acquired through the years of silent films were cast aside and forgotten in the shadow of the microphone."

5. *Finally, compose complete sentences for the intermediate categories (A, B, C, and so on):*[1]

II. At first sound inhibited the emerging art of cinema.

   A. Sound was introduced by businessmen to increase movie attendance.

   1. Attendance at movies had declined by 1926.

   2. The first talkie, *The Jazz Singer* with Al Jolsen, appeared in 1927, and by 1929 movie attendance had doubled.

   3. Arthur Knight quotes *Variety:* " 'Sound didn't do any more to the industry than turn it upside down, shake the entire bag of tricks from its pocket and advance Warner Brothers from the last place [among the film companies] to first in the league.' "

   B. Early sound films used sound excessively and artlessly.

   1. Arthur Knight: ". . . 1929 was for the most part the year of static, photographed stage plays, the year of the 'all-talking, all-singing' musical, the year which raw sound was exploited in every imaginable way."

   2. Mack Sennett's *The Family Picnic* thrilled movie goers with the exaggerated sound of picnickers eating potato chips and celery.

---

[1]Or perhaps steps 4 and 5 should be combined. Some students may find it easier to write out their intermediate categories as complete sentences *at the same time* they combine notes (step 4).

C. Early sound films lacked the fluidity of silent films.
   1. Since cameras had to be housed in soundproof booths, scenes were shot from fixed ranges and angles, and takes were very long.
   2. Ivor Montagu: "The resulting films were truly dull."
   3. Knight: "In no time at all the techniques, the artistry that directors had acquired through the years of silent films were cast aside and forgotten in the shadow of the microphone."

Sample completed working outline with notes:

Thesis: The advent of sound in 1927 at first posed a threat to the developing art of cinema, and only gradually won a place in the repertoire of editing principles established during the silent era.

I. Principles of film editing were first established during the silent-film era.
   A. The American director D. W. Griffith is generally credited with developing most of the major principles of editing still in use today.
      1. Griffith frequently filmed his scenes from a variety of ranges and angles.
      2. Griffith edited his films to vary the tempo and mood of his scenes.
      3. Griffith developed the technique of cross-cutting—advancing two lines of action at the same time.
   B. The Russian filmmakers of the silent era further explored the many possibilities of image-to-image relationships, or "montage."
      1. Lev Kuleshov's experiments demonstrated that an audience's reactions to an actor's performance depend on how footage of the actor is spliced.
      2. Sergei Eisenstein's theory of montage was based on the "third thing" principle—two pieces of film spliced together make a third thing, an effect greater than the sum of the parts.

II. At first sound inhibited the emerging art of cinema.
   A. Sound was introduced by businessmen to increase movie attendance.
      1. Attendance at movies had declined by 1926.
      2. The first talkie, *The Jazz Singer* with Al Jolsen,

appeared in 1927, and by 1929 movie attendance had doubled.

3. Arthur Knight quotes *Variety:* " 'Sound didn't do any more to the industry than turn it upside down, shake the entire bag of tricks from its pocket and advance Warner Brothers from the last place [among the film companies] to first in the league.' "

B. Early sound films used sound excessively and artlessly.

1. Arthur Knight: ". . . 1929 was for the most part the year of static, photographed stage plays, the year of the 'all-talking, all-singing' musical, the year which raw sound was exploited in every imaginable way."

2. Mack Sennett's *The Family Picnic* thrilled movie goers with the exaggerated sound of picnickers eating potato chips and celery.

C. Early sound films lacked the fluidity of silent films.

1. Since cameras had to be housed in soundproof booths, scenes were shot from fixed ranges and angles, and takes were very long.

2. Ivor Montagu: "The resulting films were truly dull."

3. Knight: "In no time at all the techniques, the artistry that directors had acquired through the years of silent films were cast aside and forgotten in the shadow of the microphone."

III. Later on, sound won a place in the repertoire of editing principles.

A. The Russian filmmakers urged that sound be used to create new montages based on image-to-sound and sound-to-sound relationships.

1. The Russian "Statement": The overuse of sound can "hinder the development and perfection of cinema as an art . . . while [it] threatens to destroy all its formal achievements."

2. The Russians proposed that the "contrapuntal" and "nonsynchronic" uses of sound be explored.

B. Filmmakers of the early thirties overcame the technical barriers to the artistic uses of sound.

1. King Vidor used postdubbing to create a sound

track after shooting his *Hallelujah!* on location in the swamps of Arkansas.

    2.   Cameras were soundproofed and became mobile again as they had been during the silent era.

  C. Some filmmakers of the thirties used sound to create new montages anticipated by Eisenstein.

    1.   Hitchcock, in his *39 Steps,* blended the sound of a woman screaming with the shriek of a locomotive (sound-to-sound montage).

    2.   In *Sous les Toits,* René Clair directed a fistfight to the sound of a passing train (sound-to-image montage).

  D. Sound no doubt increased the filmmaker's options, but experts do not agree on the relationship of sound to image.

    1.   Ivor Montagu: "... picture is primary. The problem is to find the sound to go with the picture, rather than the picture to go with the sound."

    2.   Raymond Spottiswoode: "The total film" comprises a visual and an aural factor.

    3.   Marshall McLuhan: "The hybrid or the meeting of two media is a moment of truth and revelation from which new form is born."

This outline, then, shows the relationship between specific notes taken during research and certain general ideas the researcher wants to present in his paper. In practice, rather than writing such a complete outline, you may need only write out your major entries (Roman numeral and letter entries) and arrange your notes in the same order you intend to use them in your paper. You may also want to identify each note with the number and letter of the outline entry it is keyed with. Sample note cards with outline entries identified in the upper righthand corners appear on pages 88-89.

    III D. Sound no doubt increased the filmmaker's options, but experts do not agree on the relationship of sound to image

Critiquing your outline

The better your outline, the better your finished paper will be, and the easier it will be to write. Just as your first thesis sentence was almost surely capable of refinement, so is your outline. Make sure some of those decisions you are putting off until you write your paper cannot be dealt with first by revising your outline. Time spent

Montagu, p 153   III, D, 1

"... picture is primary. The problem
is to find the sound to go
with the picture, rather
than the picture to go
with the sound."

Spottiswoode, p. 43   III, D, 2

"The total film" comprises
a visual and an aural
factor.

McLuhan, p. 63   III, D, 3

"The hybrid or the meeting of two media is a moment of truth and revelation from which new form is born."

revising the outline is always time doubly saved writing the paper. Before getting on to the writing of your paper, you might check out your outline for these common problems:

The outline advances too many main ideas, poorly related If your outline tries to advance too many main (Roman numeral) ideas, your paper could come off shallow and vague. Also, the ideas of your paper may not be well related. Example:

> *Thesis:* Like other overgrown institutions, our college system has become self-serving and wasteful, and its influence should now be restricted to allow alternatives to flourish.
>
>   I. Large industrial corporations, often in a kind of partnership with the government, now have great power to control the economy and shape public opinion to their own ends.
> II. The growth of the military, assisted by government and industry, has resulted in much waste of lives, money, and resources.
> III. As large institutions, our colleges have become self-serving and wasteful.
> IV. Our larger universities, as members of the "military-industrial complex," have subordinated teaching to the pursuit of lucrative research contracts.
>   V. The evidence suggests that grades and degrees have little bearing on job success.
> VI. The influence of colleges must be restricted to allow alternative ways of learning to flourish.

VII. Ivan Illich feels we should establish a number of alternatives to college by which people can teach themselves what they need to know.

Not all these ideas deserve Roman-numeral status. The thesis for this outline suggests that entries I and II are really members of a broader category idea:

I. Some of our institutions have grown so large as to become self-serving and wasteful.
  A. Large industrial corporations, often in a kind of partnership with the government, now have great power to control the economy and shape public opinion to their own ends.
  B. the growth of the military, assisted by government and industry, has resulted in much waste of lives, money, and resources.

Similarly, entries IV and V should be demoted to letter-entry status under entry III, renumbered II:

II. As large institutions, our colleges also have become self-serving and wasteful.
  A. Our larger universities, as members of the "military-industrial complex," have subordinated teaching to the pursuit of lucrative research contracts.
  B. The evidence suggests that grades and degrees have little bearing on job success.

Finally, entry VII is clearly a member of the category established by entry VI:

III. The influence of colleges must be restricted to allow alternative ways of learning to flourish.
  A. Ivan Illich feels we should establish a number of alternatives to college by which people can teach themselves what they need to know.

With these changes, the outline is now tighter and the relationships between category (general) ideas and member (specific) ideas are now clearer.

The main ideas of the outline have only one member idea Don't forget: If you enter an "A" you must also enter a "B." Main ideas establish categories of at least *two* member ideas. If no "B" entry for

III. The influence of colleges must be restricted to allow alternative ways of learning to flourish.
  A. Ivan Illich feels we should establish a number of alternatives to college by which people can teach themselves what they need to know.

comes to mind, entry "A" should be promoted to Roman numeral status:

III. Ivan Illich feels we should establish a number of alternatives to college by which people can teach themselves what they need to know.

Or a "B" entry will have to be added:

III. The influence of colleges must be restricted to allow alternative ways of learning to flourish.
  A. Ivan Illich feels we should establish a number of alternatives to college by which people can teach themselves what they need to know.
  B. Paul Goodman has proposed a number of measures for streamlining colleges and using the savings to subsidize alternate ways of learning.

The sections of the outline are poorly proportioned Are some sections of your outline too long or too short? This depends on the importance you place on the ideas of the various sections of your outline. Sections advancing important ideas obviously should be longer and better developed than sections advancing less important ideas. The length of the sections of your outline should be proportional to the number of pages you plan to devote to each section in your finished paper.

The rough outline about colleges so far has three sections (I, II, and III), each with two entries (A and B). But the thesis seems to stress sections II and III. Perhaps these sections need to be expanded:

II. As large institutions, our colleges also have become self-serving and wasteful.
  A. Our large universities, in joining up with the "military-industrial complex," have neglected their teaching duties to pursue lucrative research grants.
  B. As the nation's second largest industry, formal education has the muscle to promote itself and resist attempts to reform it.
  C. Colleges have a virtual monopoly on teaching and job training.
  D. The evidence suggests that grades and degrees have little bearing on job success.
  E. Higher education has become the "New World Church."
III. The influence of colleges must be restricted to allow alternative ways of learning to flourish.
  A. Americans are beginning to doubt the sanctity of the military.

B. Basic reform of our college system might also begin with an awareness of how large institutions render their clients nearly helpless to act on their own behalf.

C. Ivan Illich feels we should establish alternatives to college by which people can teach themselves what they need to know.

D. Paul Goodman has proposed streamlining colleges and using the savings to subsidize alternate ways of learning.

E. Ivar Berg has urged reassessment of "this purposeless credential consciousness."

Member-ideas are placed under the wrong category-idea It is easy to see why the entry "Volkswagens" in

I. American cars
   A. Chevrolets
   B. Volkswagens
   C. Fords

is not a member of the category "American cars." But it may be a little harder to see why the entry "E. Higher education has become the 'New World Church' " does not belong under entry "II. As large institutions, our colleges also have become self-serving and wasteful." True, both churches and colleges are institutions, but entry E does not suggest self-serving or waste, as entry II promised. Also, note how entry "A. Americans are beginning to doubt the sanctity of the military" is not a member of the category set up by "III. The influence of college must be restricted to allow alternative ways of learning to flourish."

This failure to show how member-ideas belong under category-ideas is a common problem in outlining. Several remedies are possible: (1) the out-of-place entry may have to be dropped altogether; (2) it may be placed under a more suitable category idea; (3) it may be combined with another entry that isn't out of place; or (4) it may be revised to make it a true member of its category-idea. Below, the two suspicious entries in the outline about colleges have been combined, altered somewhat, and placed under main idea III:

III. The influence of colleges must be restricted to allow alternate ways of learning to flourish.
   A. We will not find the boldness to restrict the influence of colleges until we first desanctify them, just as we are beginning to doubt the sanctity of the military and scale down its operations.

Finally, if you can stand one more run-through, here is the outline refined enough to begin writing the paper. (Specific notes have been omitted.)

Thesis: Like other overgrown institutions, our college system has become self-serving and wasteful, and its influence should now be restricted to allow alternatives to flourish.

I. Large institutions in general often become self-serving and wasteful.
    A. Large industrial corporations, with the help of the government, now have great power to control the economy and shape public opinion to their own ends.
    B. The growth of the military, assisted by government and industry, has resulted in much waste of lives, money, and resources.

II. As large institutions, our colleges also have become self-serving and wasteful.
    A. Our leading universities have neglected their teaching duties to conduct lucrative research projects for the so-called military-industrial complex.
    B. As the nation's second largest industry, big education has the muscle to promote itself and resist attempts to reform it.
    C. Colleges have a virtual monopoly on teaching and job training.
    D. The evidence suggests that grades and degrees have little bearing on job success.

III. The influence of colleges must be restricted to allow alternative ways of learning to flourish.
    A. We will not find the boldness to restrict the influence of colleges until we first desanctify them, just as we are beginning to doubt the sanctity of the military and scale down its operations.
    B. Basic reform of our college system might also begin with an awareness of how large institutions render their clients nearly helpless to act on their own behalf.
    C. Ivan Illich feels we should establish alternatives to college by which people can teach themselves what they need to know.
    D. Paul Goodman has proposed streamlining colleges and using the savings to subsidize alternate ways of learning.
    E. Ivar Berg has urged reassessment of "this purposeless credential consciousness."

The Longer Paper

Using the main ideas of your refined thesis as a guide, develop an outline that is complete enough to allow you to write your paper. Check your outline to make sure: (a) it does not advance too many main ideas; (b) all main or category ideas have at least two member ideas; (c) the sections of the outline are properly proportioned; (d) member ideas are placed under the most appropriate category ideas.

Activities

1. Develop the main ideas in each of the following theses into Roman numeral entries of an outline. Write each entry as a complete sentence and arrange the entries in a best order. Example:

    Thesis: Mountain climbing not only offers many challenges in an era of declining challenges, it also puts us in touch with nature just when man seems most separated from nature.

    I.   We live in an era of declining challenges.
    II. Mountain climbing offers many challenges.
    III. We also seem to have separated ourselves from nature.
    IV. Mountain climbing puts us in touch with nature again.

    A. Since most teenagers are emotionally immature and financially insecure, they are seldom ready for marriage.
    B. The influence of the family may have declined in recent years, but its role as a teacher and basic provider for the very young will never be replaced.
    C. If the sale and use of marijuana is ever legalized, the government should regulate its sales and underwrite further research into its effects.
    D. Two aspects of existentialism, its insistence on paradox and its preoccupation with anxiety, make it unlikely that this philosophy will ever be embraced by great numbers of people.
    E. Although both the Israeli and hippie-style communes were founded as alternatives to capitalist societies, the Israeli groups have developed self-government further than the looser American groups have.

2. Fill in the blanks (or write out on your own paper):
    I.   Occupations
         A. Public service
             1. Teaching
             2. _____
             3. _____
         B. Technical and professional
             1. Engineering
             2. _____
             3. _____
    I.   _____
         A. Trailers
             1. Self-contained
             2. _____

B. _____
   1. Pup tents
   2. _____
C. _____
   1. _____
   2. _____

I. How to succeed in college
  A. _____
    1. _____
    2. _____
  B. _____
    1. _____
    2. _____

Thesis: A year of well-planned travel can be very educational.

I. Travel can be planned
  A. State and local chambers of commerce will mail literature on request.
  B. _____
II. Planned travel can be educational
  A. Travel teaches history
  B. _____
  C. _____

Thesis: The role of women in society has changed dramatically during the past fifty years.

I. Fifty years ago woman's place was in the home.
  A. _____
    1. _____
    2. _____
  B. _____
    1. _____
    2. _____
II. _____
  A. _____
    1. _____
    2. _____
  B. _____
    1. _____
    2. _____

Thesis: If college life were not so impersonal, students would learn better and enjoy themselves more.

I. _____
  A. _____
  B. _____
II. _____
  A. _____
  B. _____
III. _____
  A. _____
  B. _____

3. Select a topic from the list below:
  A. Religious fanatics.
  B. Your favorite sport.

C. Billboards.
D. The attitudes of youth toward war.
E. Draft counseling.
F. Your job (or future job).
G. Child beating.
H. A neglected social problem.
I. A TV show that made you sick.
J. Alternatives to college.
K. A topic of your choice.

Next, pose a thesis for your topic. Write an outline from your thesis, critique and rewrite the outline if necessary.

4. Write a short paper based on the outline your wrote for activity 3.

8
Writing the Paper

Millions of literate people conduct informal research all the time by reading whatever newspapers, magazines, and books come their way; but few of these people actually write papers before deciding about which political candidate to vote for or which career to embark on. Research need not end in the writing of a paper to be useful. If for some reason you don't write your paper, you might flunk the course in which the paper was required, but your research would not have been a waste of time, considering all you learned.

But writing a paper based on your findings can add to the value of research, and not just for the grade. Writing helps you find your best ideas. It chases out vague notions from the back of your mind and gives them shape and substance. Writing a paper fixes your ideas, permanently, in ink. The finished paper is something you can point to and say, "There. Now my ideas are down on paper. I know my mind." And writing captures your best ideas on paper as much for yourself as for other people who might be interested.

From outline to paper

Your task now is to flesh out your outline, to transform it into a paper. The outline should show the relationships among most of the ideas that will appear in your paper, but the writing of the paper itself, the setting down of sentences and paragraphs, presents new problems. Below are some strategies for completing the transformation from outline to paper.

The introduction Many kinds of writing have a three-part structure, and so should your paper: a brief introduction, a much longer body or middle section, and a brief conclusion. The purpose of the introduction is to ease your reader into your paper and present him with your thesis. But an outline usually makes no provision for an introduction; it is meant instead to guide the writing of the body of the paper where the thesis is developed. If you feel your outline doesn't help you too much in writing an introduction, try one or more of these strategies:

1. *Attract your reader's attention.* An introduction often may be

based on an anecdote, a question, a quotation, or a little-known fact or statistic that creates interest.

2. *Justify the topic you are writing about.* An introduction might also mention why the topic the paper will explore is worth writing about, why the reader should read the paper at all.

3. *Narrow your topic.* An introduction may also serve as a sort of funnel, first presenting broad and general ideas the reader is familiar with before narrowing to the more restricted topic the paper treats.

4. *At first be rather obvious and agreeable.* The opening sentences of an introduction often express rather obvious and agreeable sentiments about the topic of the paper before coming to the thesis, which usually deals with less well-known or even controversial ideas. This strategy is meant to put your reader into a favorable frame of mind before presenting him with your thesis.

All these strategies really have one purpose: to lead up to the thesis and prepare the reader for it. Your introduction should *conclude* with your thesis.

Sample introduction with thesis in italics:

The advent of the optical sound track in the late 1920s was probably the single most important technical development for advancing the art of film since 1889 when George Eastman finally succeeded in coating strips of celluloid with photographic emulsion. Before sound, of course, filmmakers had to say everything in pictures; with sound the filmmakers' options were increased considerably. And no technical breakthrough since sound—color, wide screen, stereoptic photography—has had quite the same impact. But what many modern moviegoers don't realize, perhaps, is that the advent of sound was not exactly welcomed by most serious filmmakers of the time. *In fact, sound at first actually posed a threat to the developing art of cinema, and only gradually won a place in the repertoire of editing principles first established during the silent-film era.*

Background material Nearly all research papers include some background material. This could be a brief summary of issues, a glance into the past, an explanation of terms, or an accounting of crucial facts or developments. If, during the writing of your paper, you decide you should include some background material for your reader, a good place to insert this information is after the introduction. However, if your thesis depends heavily on background material, you may decide to scatter this throughout the body of your paper. Here is a paragraph of background material for a paper exploring the impact of sound on the later development of motion picture art.

Filmmakers have always been interested in exploring the technical aspects of their art. But the introduction of the optical sound track in 1927 was the brainchild of the businessmen who ran the great Hollywood studios, and was intended more to stimulate movie attendance than to advance the art of film. It worked. Paid admission to movies nearly doubled in the three years following the release of *The Jazz Singer,* the first feature-length movie to use the new sound system.

Warning: Too much background material when it is unnecessary for advancing the thesis looks like padding to achieve a minimum page requirement. Keep your presentation of background material as brief as possible. If your thesis deals with the dangers of LSD, your reader doesn't need four pages about how LSD was first synthesized by Swiss chemists. A half page or so of background material is usually all your reader will tolerate; he wants you to get on with your thesis.

The body: developing paragraphs from outline entries   After writing your introduction and supplying whatever background material you think is crucial, you can turn now to your outline for help in writing the body of your paper. You should be able to develop most of the paragraphs of the body of your paper from the entries of your outline. Often you can combine a main or category entry with several minor or member entries to develop a paragraph. Example:

Outline: category idea and member ideas:

A.   The American director D. W. Griffith has been credited with developing most of the major principles of editing still in use today.

  1.   Griffith frequently filmed his scenes from a variety of ranges and angles.

  2.   Griffith edited his films to vary the tempo and mood of his scenes.

  3.   Griffith developed the technique of cross-cutting— advancing two lines of action at the same time.

Paragraph:

Knight credits the American silent-era director D. W. Griffith with developing most of the editing principles still in use today. It was Griffith who first understood that scenes could be presented from different ranges and angles, something the stage play could never do. Griffith also discovered that much unimportant action could be cut to tighten the stream of events, just as the length of many shots could be shortened or lengthened to affect mood and tempo. Finally, Griffith also developed the technique of cross-cutting, or advancing two or more lines of action at the same time. All of these techniques helped film find an identity apart from the stage play.

The italicized sentence of the paragraph represents the main outline entry A and serves as a sort of miniature thesis to control the rest of the paragraph. Sentences that control paragraphs this way are often called *topic sentences.* (Incidentally, this paragraph also shows the flexible relationship between the outline and the paper. The outline was incomplete in that it made no mention of how film compares to the stage play, an idea that occurred to the writer as he wrote the paragraph.)

Often a paragraph may have to be written from but a single entry of the outline. In this case, the writer has notes available to help him flesh out the paragraph:

Outline entry:

1. Lev Kuleshov's experiments demonstrated that an audience's reaction to an actor's performance depends on how footage of the actor is spliced.

Paragraph:

During the 1920s, Russian filmmakers experimented extensively with the basic principles Griffith developed. Lev Kuleshov, for instance, obtained close-up footage of an expressionless male actor. To this footage he spliced first a shot of a bowl of soup, then a shot of a child playing with a stuffed animal, and finally a dead women in a coffin. Audiences to whom the spliced footage was shown raved about the actor's performances. Never had they seen such an expression of hunger, such fatherly affection, such grief. *As Knight explains, "it is not merely the image alone, but the juxtaposition of images that creates the emotional tone of a sequence."*

In this paragraph, either the first sentence or the closing quotation serves as a topic sentence. Topic sentences can occur anywhere in a paragraph, although they are frequently opening sentences. Some paragraphs need no topic sentences at all; they convey a sense of unity or wholeness without relying on a single sentence that generalizes about the paragraph.

A few paragraphs you write may not be based on any outline entries at all. Such paragraphs have several purposes: (1) they summarize or point out the importance of earlier paragraphs based on the outline; (2) they serve as bridges between major sections of the paper; (3) or they contain your personal views on the findings you present. The paragraph below combines all three functions: It comments on findings presented earlier, it bridges two sections of the paper, and it expresses the personal views of the writer. The paragraph was not suggested by any particular outline entry, but rather occurred to the writer as he wrote his paper.

In my view, gluts of anything have a way of making people think twice. Too many weapons and casualties of war have produced genuine popular movements to cut back the military. Too many cars have spurred people to consider alternate means of transportation. Too many college graduates who may not find the jobs they think they deserve will, I maintain, move the nation to scale down its wasteful system of college education while exploring alternatives to college for learning and job training.

Additional examples of developing paragraphs from outline entries:

> *Outline of a paragraph combining quotations from two different sources:*
> C. Early sound films lacked the fluidity of silent films.
>   1. Since cameras had to be housed in soundproof booths, scenes were shot from fixed ranges and angles, and takes were very long.
>   2. Montagu: "The resulting films were truly dull."
>   3. Knight: "In no time at all the techniques, the artistry that directors had acquired through years of silent films were cast aside and forgotten in the shadow of the microphone."
>
> *Paragraph:*

The camera, once mobile, now had to be enclosed in a soundproof booth so the sound of its whirling gears would not be picked up by the microphone. Scenes could no longer be shot from changing ranges and angles. Visually, "The resulting films," writes Montagu, "were truly dull." It was almost as if film art had retreated to pre-Griffith days. Knight laments, "In no time at all the techniques, the artistry that directors had acquired through the years of silent films were cast aside and forgotten in the shadow of the microphone."

> *Outline of two paragraphs of statistical material, personal opinion, and a quotation:*
> B. As the nation's second largest industry, big education has the muscle to promote itself and resist attempts to reform it.
>   1. Higher education.
>   a. $10 billion a year.
>   b. Annual growth rate 10 percent.
>   c. Half million employees, seven million students.
>   2. Education overall.
>   a. $58 billion annually.
>   b. Second only to Defense.
>   c. 60 million students and employees.
>   3. David Hapgood: "The escalating demand for diplomas in the marketplace has made education a huge, sluggish beast, as alert and competitive as a grass-eating dinosaur. . . . Blessed with a monopoly on diplomas and the fastest growth rate in the na-

tion, the industry is under no pressure to change. It does not have to hustle its clients. The product sells itself."

Paragraphs:

Our college system as a whole must be viewed as a big business. Colleges and universities operate on revenues of $10 billion a year with an annual growth rate of 10 percent. Over two thousand institutions of higher learning employ half a million people and hold about seven million students. But this is only part of the story. Nearly all of our primary and secondary schools are geared, in various ways, to mesh with the college system. Overall, Americans spend $58 billion annually on formal education. The only institution that spends more is the Defense Department. Over a fourth of our population—60 million youngsters and adults—are connected full-time with the knowledge industry.

In my view, big education has the muscle to promote itself while resisting challenges to reform it. The danger is that higher education, like the military, has become a self-validating, self-perpetuating system with almost no external checks on its growth and influence. This seems to be the point of view of David Hapgood, a senior research fellow at New York University, who has written:

> The escalating demand for diplomas in the marketplace has made education a huge, sluggish beast, as alert and competitive as a grass-eating dinosaur. ... Blessed with a monopoly on diplomas and the fastest growth rate in the nation, the industry is under no pressure to change. It does not have to hustle its clients. The product sells itself.

The conclusion The conclusion, like the introduction, is brief. It too is seldom accounted for in the outline. The conclusion may simply summarize important ideas of the paper, but usually it tries to show what the thesis of the paper *means,* or what is implied beyond the limits of the paper. Below is a conclusion for a paper that developed a thesis dealing with the wastefulness of colleges and the need to explore alternatives.

These proposals, I believe, would break the colleges' present monopoly on teaching and job training and allow viable alternatives to flourish. Whoever elected to attend college would do so out of choice, not necessity. The new bare-bones colleges would become true centers of learning rather than places to accumulate credits and degrees. The colleges would have to compete for clients, and the competition would render them more efficient and responsive. We Americans generally hold that competition of this sort is healthy; why shouldn't it improve our colleges as well?.

Presenting quoted material

Much of the success of your finished paper will turn on how artfully you used quoted material to advance your ideas. Treated gracefully, quotations can enhance your paper; treated clumsily, they will soon drive your reader away.

Avoiding lengthy quotations: summary and ellipsis marks You will want, of course, to use your best quotations in defense of your ideas. If a person you read said something with insight, eloquence, or wit, by all means quote him. Quote him especially if he says things you couldn't begin to express as well. But like overlong background presentations, too-lengthy quotations may turn the reader against you. He suspects you don't really have much to say yourself and you need long quotations to fill in the gaps in your thinking and reach the required number of pages. You should pare away nonessential sentences and quote only the best of a man's writing. Consider the following lengthy quotation:

The nation's armed forces are supported by a vast and permanent arms industry and a complex of related interests which affect thousands of communities and millions of Americans. These Americans—in uniform, veterans of military service, defense-industry employees and their dependents, defense scientists, Defense Department civilians, businessmen and politicians—all have direct and personal interests in the nature and scope of militarism and the activities of the defense establishment. How did this militaristic society evolve? How did "peace-loving" America become a colossal war machine?

Our military power ostensibly has been intended only to defend the nation and to help protect its friends and allies from attack, yet it has become the cause of much national dissension and disagreement. It is the reason for a good deal of American unpopularity abroad. Our military power has come to be viewed by many people as a self-perpetuating force of aggression and destruction motivated by many interests beyond the needs of national defense. It has led us into the most disliked and controversial war of our history and has isolated the United States from its traditional allies and the peoples of the world.

This quotation might be pared down by summarizing its ideas and quoting only a few key phrases and sentences:

James A. Donovan, a retired Marine Corps colonel, feels that numerous defense-related organizations and groups have a direct interest in expanding the role of the military. The result, according to Donovan, is that the United States has become "a colossal war machine" producing unrest at home and a loss of prestige for the United States abroad. Donovan comments: "Our military power has come to be viewed by many people as a self-perpetuating force of aggression and destruction motivated by many interests beyond the needs of national defense."

Another way to condense lengthy quotations is by *the use of ellipsis marks.* Ellipsis marks are three periods in a row (. . .), and indicate that portions of quoted material have been omitted. These omissions might be single words, phrases, or entire sentences in a sequence of sentences. Here is a condensed version of the longer passage about the military, with ellipsis marks to show deletions:

The nation's armed forces are supported by a vast and permanent arms industry and a complex of related interests. . . . These Americans . . . have direct and personal interests in the nature and scope of militarism. . . . Our military power has come to be viewed by many people as a self-perpetuating force of aggression and destruction motivated by many interests beyond the needs of national defense. It has led us into the most disliked . . . war of our history and has isolated the United States from . . . the peoples of the world.

The elliptical version may not be as subtle as the original, but it is more to the point.

More frequently, however, ellipsis marks are used for omitting portions of a quotation which are irrelevant or even distracting. Example:

Original passage:

There is, in fact, an absence of evidence that the most able in performance of jobs or other real-life tasks are selected or produced by the standards set and training offered by higher education.

The passage as quoted with "in fact" omitted:

Sociologist Patricia Sexton has written: "There is . . . an absence of evidence that the most able in performance of jobs or other real-life tasks are selected or produced by the standards set and training offered by higher education."

Because "in fact" in this passage made little sense out of context, it was left out of the quoted version.

Clarifying quoted material: using brackets It is also permissible to insert your own words into quoted material if you feel certain clarifications or alterations are necessary. Enclose your editorial additions in brackets [ ] instead of parentheses ( ) since the original might have included parentheses.[1] Bracketed insertions are often used for clarifying pronouns whose referents have not been picked up in your quotation:

What are the chances that Americans will scale down their military and make its operations more sensible? Not good, according to Donovan. He writes: " . . . this [the spread of militarism] is happening not as a result of a deliberate choice by the American people, but as a result of an accumula-

---

[1]Brackets may be made on a typewriter by a combination of slashes and under-strokes: $\lceil \quad \rfloor$.

tion of military decisions, commitments, and actions that are beyond the control of the present democratic process."

Or for other clarifications necessary because of limited context:

Knight describes how Mack Sennett's comedy *The Family Picnic* "regaled [audiences] by the sounds of the picnickers crunching celery or munching potato chips."

Or for minor alterations to improve readability:

The Russian filmmakers, while recognizing that sound was here to stay, warned that its overuse could "hinder the development and perfection of cinema as an art [while it] threatens to destroy all its present formal achievements."

Minimizing distortion when quoting When you tinker with quoted material, make sure you don't end up with ideas the writer himself would deny he meant. The material you choose to delete should not contain important ifs, buts, or on-the-other-hands that significantly qualify a writer's main line of thought. Nor should your bracketed insertions alter the overall meaning of a passage you want to quote. Edit quoted material only to condense or clarify; never, never make these changes to bend the thought of a passage to suit your purposes. If in doubt, quote as fully as necessary to preserve the writer's original intent.

Leading into quoted material The graceful writer varies his lead-ins to the material he quotes. Here are several strategies for linking your running text with your quotations:

1. *Complete sentence before quotation.* A complete sentence that leads into a quotation should end with a colon (:):

Sociologist Patricia Sexton has written about the relationship of college training to job performance: "There is . . . an absence of evidence that the most able in performance of jobs or other real-life tasks are selected or produced by the standards set and training offered by higher education."

2. *Lead-in and quotation combine to make a single sentence.* Here several approaches are possible:

   Short lead-in phrase with comma:

According to Sexton, "Employers often hire from among the degree elite because of the prestige rather than the superior training or job performance skill attached to a college degree."

As Knight explains, "It is not merely the image alone, but the juxtaposition of images that creates the emotional tone of a sequence."

   "That" before quotation:

Ivan Illich, a priest interested in educational reform, feels that "the New World Church is the knowledge industry."

As characters speak the camera fixes on other characters and objects so that "the sound acts as a rhythmic counterpoint link to the jump-rhythm of the images succeeding each other."

Lead-in and quotation form a single, blended thought:

Knight describes the best silent films as having "created a world of persuasive reality despite the absence of voices and the verifying clangor of natural sound."

Paul Goodman thinks the colleges should "drop mandarin requirements of academic diplomas that are irrelevant, and rid [themselves] of the ridiculous fad of awarding diplomas for every skill and trade whatever."

3. *Splitting a quoted sentence.* Another alternative is to split a sentence you want to quote and let the first half serve as a lead-in:

"The escalating demand for diplomas in the marketplace," writes David Hapgood, "has made education a huge, sluggish beast, as alert and competitive as a grass-eating dinosaur."

Visually, "The resulting films," writes Montagu, "were truly dull."

4. *Sprinkling a summary with key words and phrases from a quotation.* Summaries often capture the flavor of the original better if they draw on certain key words and phrases from the original passage:

Ridgeway maintains that the modern university exists primarily to carry out war-related research and to provide professors launching pads to orbit their lucrative careers in advising industry. Learning and job training do not figure prominently in Ridgeway's portrait of the university. Undergraduates lie in "holding pens" and are useful, in Ridgeway's view, primarily for financing the university. Graduate students act as baby sitters for "keeping the undergraduates in hand" while "assisting the senior professors in carrying forward their inquiries." The name of the game is to make sure that "money flows out of the government down to the university, where someone hatches a utilitarian idea, and from there [the money flows] over to a company which either makes a product or designs a test."

Most of these devices for setting up quotations apply only to shorter quoted passages—a sentence or part of a sentence. Longer quotations are usually preceded by complete sentences ending in a colon.

Giving credit

Most of these examples of lead-ins to quotations include the name of the writer and a tagline about his profession or claim to authority. This information helps your reader judge the worth of the quotations you use. Quotations that are not attributed to their authors are very confusing to the reader. He can't be sure a series of quotations you present was written by one writer or several. Even if your text does say who wrote a certain passage you quote, your reader may want to know who the writer is, what gave him the right to sound off. Taglines suggest the writer's claim to authority. Examples:

James A. Donovan, a retired Marine Corps colonel, has written: " ... "

Sociologist Patricia Sexton has written about the relationship of college training to job performance: " ... "

Ivan Illich, a priest interested in educational reform, feels that " ... "

Your summaries, too, should be sprinkled with the name of the writer whose ideas you are using:

Illich wants to eliminate what he feels is the wasteful middleman, the school or college with all its buildings, files, business dealings, support personnel, marching bands, and football teams. He believes we should put dollars we normally spend on inefficient schooling into the hands of people, young and old, poor and not so poor, so they can seek whatever training they think they need from free-lancing teachers and working professionals. Illich apparently has faith that people, once liberated from overgrown institutions, can act sensibly on their own behalf and teach themselves what they need to know to become self-sufficient.

At the same time, the reader wants to know where your own ideas begin; your opinions should be clearly labeled as such:

As for myself, I would propose two remedies, one economic, the other legal. I would first channel most funds now spent on the present wasteful college system into creating new institutions of learning along the lines of the proposals of Illich, Goodman, and Berg. Secondly, I would enact laws to phase out many questionable diploma and credential programs. I agree with Illich that it should be illegal to judge an applicant's worth on the basis of prior schooling. In my opinion, the sole criteria for hiring should be skill, knowledge, and demonstrated potential, and it should not matter where or how the applicant developed these qualities.

Avoiding plagiarism

Plagiarism is an ugly word like plague or maim or snot. It stands for the worst sin a writer can commit—copying out someone else's writing and passing it off as his own. True plagiarism is executed with full knowledge of one's dishonesty. A writer claims to have written what he lets other people read when he knows perfectly well he did not. The sentences, the phrases he used were lifted from a book or article and set down word for word, comma by comma, in his paper *without quotation marks.* The paper usually reads pretty well because the person he stole from is a pro—else he wouldn't have been published in the first place.

True plagiarism can get you into all kinds of trouble. At best, the teacher who catches a student at it will probably lower the grade of his paper. Many teachers stop reading at the first sure sign of plagiarism and draw a big red "F" on the title page. At worst, students who plagiarize have been known to flunk courses and get kicked out of college. As a rule, plagiarists are shunned by society. They cast no shadow on the ground. Dogs bark at them as they pass, and small children cast stones at them.

Such is the nature and fate of true plagiarists. But there are degrees of plagiarism. Some students, in fact, commit plagiarism without being aware of it. They do not understand the difference between *copying* and *composing*. They think that writing a research paper is copying down verbatim material from their sources. They don't understand that writing is composing, thinking up their own sentences with their own phrases, words, and marks of punctuation. They don't see that writing—composing—is art, and that they shouldn't steal another man's writing and sign their names to it any more than they would steal paintings and claim to have painted them.

Other students apparently feel it is all right to copy out straightforward technical or factual reports and set them down in their research papers as if they had written them. There is little art or high thought involved in describing the effects of smoking on the lungs; why should students bother with putting it all in their own words when *Time* or the *A.M.A. Journal* said it so much better? But summaries of factual material are often better than word-for-word accounts because they can save space and are sometimes more to the point. Moreover, technical writing is indeed an art, or at least a respectable skill, and the man who writes up reports well should be given credit for his pains.

Still other students think they can escape being charged with plagiarism by changing a few words of a passage—"believes" to "feels," or "finally" to "in conclusion"—before setting it down in a paper without quotation marks. But to alter a few words or phrases of a passage can hardly be considered the equivalent of writing a summary in the student's own words. And then there are students who, if they don't steal whole sentences or paragraphs, lift a well-turned phrase now and then. But that apt phrase a student seizes is no less a work of art than a well-wrought sentence. If it must be used, it should be set in quotation marks. There is, however, no hard line between certain eloquent phrases and certain set or stock phrases that have passed into the craft of sentence writing long ago and are now fair game for all writers. Expressions such as "contrary to current mythology" or "generate more heat than light" or "the arena of public opinion" are so widely used as to no longer "belong" to any one writer, and you may use them without quotation marks if you think they lend your writing sophistication.

Similarly, it is not plagiarism to borrow the special words or terms a writer uses if these are generally known to be associated with a certain issue or area of study. Words like "upwardly mobile" from the field of sociology or "military-industrial complex" associated with the issue of defense spending or "montage" from film art are fair game for all writers, even though posed originally by individual writers. Your teacher wants you to read to improve your vocabulary and level of information and to learn the special terms associated with your research topic. If your reading yielded a wealth of new words or terms, by all means use them in your paper. You'll communicate better.

Finally, some clever plagiarists don't steal sentences but instead steal ideas. They are careful to write—compose—their own sentences, but the ideas they present really belong to other people, and they damn well know it. But again, like stock phrases, ideas have a way of flowing into the mainstream so that we lose track of their origins. We forget (or never know) who first said such and such. The important thing is your own knowledge of the sources of your ideas. If you can nail an idea down to a certain man, you should give him credit for it.

If you are still unclear about how to avoid plagiarism, try these remedies:

1. Write your summaries with the sources you are using—a book, a magazine article, note cards—*out of sight.* This way you must rely on your own words. Feel free, of course, to consult your sources to get clear about them, but close the book or magazine or turn your notes over as you actually write.

2. If you simply can't write your summary with your sources out of sight, plan to *use quotation marks around any three words in a row* from another person's writing you feel you must use. If you discover that nearly all of what you have written has quotation marks around it, you haven't really written a summary.

Rewriting and proofreading

Few writers, not even professionals, get it right the first time around. You'll probably need to revise your first draft to some extent in order to communicate your ideas with clarity and grace. You should budget your time so as to save out a few days for revision and proofreading before the deadline for the finished paper descends on you. Here are some suggestions for improving your first draft:

1. If your schedule permits, stick your first draft away in a drawer and forget about it for a few days or a week. Cool off. Then pull your paper out and read it again in an objective frame of mind. Pretend you are someone else, a reader who knows very little about your research question, your reading and note-taking, your many thoughts and insights and turns of mind. Did you get it all in your paper for him? Can he follow your thoughts, or did you leave out important ideas or pieces of information? The point: revise from the *reader's* standpoint.

2. Check out your style. Good writing is clear and uncluttered writing, although it may deal with complex ideas. Cut long, mushy, gray words or expressions and substitute clear and simple words wherever possible. Also cut all unnecessary words and phrases and take the most direct route. Don't let your style of writing come between your reader and your ideas. Regard style as a means to an end, a window on your ideas. Keep the window clean. The reader is more interested in what the window reveals than in the window itself.

3. Check out the connections between your ideas. Make sure your ideas *are* connected. Avail yourself of the ordinary but valuable words and expressions in the language meant to help people connect ideas, words like *but, and, another, indeed, next, finally, if, moreover,* and *thus;* expressions like *in fact, in order to, as a result, in addition, instead of, to be sure, on the contrary,* and *on the other hand.* Get rid of the notion that you can't begin sentences with *and, but,* or *so.*

4. Check your paper for accuracy. Have you quoted correctly? Are your facts and statistics accurate? Have you summarized or edited quoted material with a minimum of distortion?

5. Proofread for correct spelling, grammar, usage, and punctuation. Spend a solid hour going over your paper with a dictionary, and a writer's guide, if you have one. Look closely at words, commas, phrases. You may have the best ideas in the world but if your writing is marred by repeated errors in mechanics and grammar, your reader won't be very sympathetic. Don't blow it all at the very end of your research project by failing to set aside time for careful proofreading.

6. Before writing a final draft, read the next chapter carefully. It deals with certain conventions of research-based writing that readers expect you to practice.

The Longer Paper

Write your paper. Follow your outline, but deviate from it if you have to. Supply a suitable introduction that prepares your reader for your thesis. Include any necessary sentences or paragraphs of transition. Add a brief conclusion that summarizes or suggests broader implications. Vary your lead-ins to quoted material. Be sure, too, to separate your ideas from those of the writers you use. Revise and proofread your first draft.

Activities

1. Develop separate paragraphs for (A), (B), (C), and (D) below:
   (A) I. How to decide on a "major" in college.
       A. See a counselor.
       B. Take a test to survey your occupational interests.
       C. Take a variety of courses and pursue your interests.
       D. Drop out of school, bum around, think, and reenroll next fall.
   (B) I. Fifty years ago woman's place was in the home.
   (C) A. The great migration.
       1. 1800: 2½ percent of the world's population lived in cities.
       2. 1970: 25 percent.
       3. 2000: 50 percent.
   (D) A. It is difficult to estimate how many people die of starvation.
       1. Statistics are incomplete.
       2. Malnutrition makes people susceptible to other diseases.
       3. Paul Ehrlich: "Deaths from starvation go unnoticed, even when they occur as close as Mississippi."
       4. *The New Republic:* 5 million children in India die from the effects of starvation every year.

2. Write a suitable introduction for one of the following thesis sentences:
   a. A year of well-planned travel can be very educational.
   b. The role of women in society has changed dramatically during the past fifty years.
   c. If college life were not so impersonal, students would learn better and enjoy themselves more.

3. If you were to write a conclusion for an essay based on one of the thesis sentences of activity 2, what broader implications might you mention?

4. Select any three topics from the list below and write a paragraph for each. Begin each paragraph with a topic sentence that serves as a sort of thesis or main idea to control the rest of the sentences.
   Topics:
   A. What is a good movie?
   B. A person you admire.
   C. Grades and learning.
   D. The end of the world.
   E. Releasing aggressions.
   F. Who says animals are dumb?

G. The value of music.
H. What went wrong with your research project?
I. Getting acquainted with people.
J. Why you want to be a ———.
K. What you didn't do last summer.
L. Why you didn't do what you didn't do last summer.
M. How you might do what you didn't do last summer next summer.
N. Three topics of your choice.

Sample paragraph with topic sentence italicized:

A good movie is one that accomplishes what film does well—evokes subtle feelings and moods through pictures. In a good film the environment or setting is important. The camera catches significant details or charges the setting with meaning for the characters or the theme. A good film also exploits the close-up shot. A screen that is filled with an actor's face can reveal much about character through a twitch of a cheek muscle or a movement of the lips. Good movies don't need a lot of dialogue, and too much talking distracts from the visual aspect of film. Rather it is the cameraman, and the director he works with, who is most responsible for producing a good film.

5. Go over the notes you took for your longer paper and
   a. Summarize the longest quotation.
   b. Prune down the longest quotation by omitting less crucial phrases and sentences. Use ellipsis marks to indicate deletions.
   c. Pull out a number of shorter quotations and practice each of the lead-in techniques discussed on pages 105 and 106.
   d. Return to the summary you wrote for item a above and sprinkle it with key words and phrases from the quotation it was based on.

9

Format for the Finished Paper

Wait! You're not through yet. Your paper may not communicate as well as it could unless you take the trouble to put it all into a respectable format. Format means appearance. Many generations of researchers have developed certain conventions for presenting their findings. A few of these conventions are rather silly, perhaps, but most of them serve useful purposes and are meant to help you reach your reader better. This chapter deals with these conventions.

Systems of documentation

Documenting means "backing up" your assertions by telling your reader where you found your facts, figures, quotations, and so forth. Even if the text of your paper mentions the names of the writers you read and their claims to authority, your reader may want more complete information about the actual books and magazines you drew on. He may want to get his hands on the same material. He may want to know if a certain article is up to date. He may want to know where exactly you found the statistics you present. Through your courtesy in supplying him with the necessary bibliographic information, he can find the materials you used or make judgments about them. There are several ways to document your sources. Here are three systems you might consider:

Footnoting   This system of documentation is the one most closely associated with the library research paper and with scholarly writing in general. It involves three steps, of which the actual footnote is but the second. The first step is the insertion of a raised number in your text wherever you feel documentation is needed. The second step is the footnote itself, found either at the bottom of the page or at the end of the paper (if at the end of the paper, called a "note"). This footnote contains all pertinent bibliographic information about the source, including the exact page number of the information you cite. The third step is the entry in the bibliography for the source. The bibliography, found at the end of the paper, is a list of all the sources you used to write your paper. To illustrate:

Step 1. Raised number in text:

Paid attendance to movies nearly doubled
in the three years following the release of
The Jazz Singer, the first feature-length
movie to use the new sound system.[1]

Step 2. Footnote:

[1]Arthur Knight. The Liveliest Art,
Mentor Books, 1957, p. 142.

Step 3. Bibliographic entry:

Knight, Arthur. The Liveliest Art, Mentor
   Books, 1957.

For a finished paper using footnotes, see pages 135 through 145.

Parenthetical references   The footnoting system has a lot of class and tradition behind it, but it does tend to be redundant. The bibliography repeats nearly all the information of the footnotes. Accordingly, some scholars have dropped footnoting for a more streamlined system of documentation known as parenthetical referencing. This system bypasses the second step, the footnote, and takes the reader directly from the text to the bibliography. It does this by inserting in the text *in place of the raised number of the footnoting system* two numbers enclosed in parentheses, for example, (4:142). The first number, 4, refers to a numbered entry in the bibliography; the second number, 142, is the page number of the source you got your information from. To illustrate:

Step 1. Parenthetical reference in text:

Paid attendance to movies nearly doubled
in the three years following the release of
The Jazz Singer, the first feature-length
movie to use the new sound system. (4:142)

Step 2. Bibliographic entry:

4.   Knight, Arthur. The Liveliest Art, Mentor
        Books, 1957.

For a finished paper using parenthetical references, see pages 146 through 161.

Textual documentation   If you are fairly certain your reader will not want complete bibliographic information about your sources, you may not need to use any of this apparatus for documentation —footnotes, parenthetical references, or bibliographies. Instead, merely anticipate the questions your reader might have about your sources and try to answer them *in your written text* by supplying whatever bibliographic information you think is crucial. Examples:

1. Suppose you want to work the title of the book into your text:

In his book The Liveliest Art, film historian
Arthur Knight has pointed out that paid attendance to movies nearly doubled in the three
years following the release of The Jazz Singer,
the first feature-length movie to use the new
sound system.

2. Your text might also mention names of magazines or newspapers:

A recent editorial in The Fresno Bee called
attention to the shortage of liveable, low-
cost housing for the poor of Fresno County.

3. If certain statistics you present are debatable, you had better say where you found your statistics:

The Fresno Bee estimates that over 60,000
residents of Fresno County live in substandard
dwellings.

4. Textual documentation may also include page numbers, if you feel these are important:

In his book The Liveliest Art, film historian
Arthur Knight has pointed out that paid attendance at movies nearly doubled in the three
years following the release of The Jazz Singer,
the first feature-length movie to use the new
sound system. (p. 142)

A bibliography may also be added. But too much apparatus defeats the purpose of textual documentation—to streamline the presentation of bibliographic information. If for whatever reason you feel your written text does not supply enough information about your sources, or if your text tends to become overburdened with information, you had better go to footnoting or parenthetical referencing. For a finished paper using textual documentation, see pages 162 through 165.

Which system of documentation should you use? That may depend as much on the nature of your paper as on your personality. If you tend to be traditionally minded, enjoy detail, or plan to do graduate work, perhaps you'll prefer footnoting. If you fancy yourself something of a free spirit and feel that exact page numbers and letter-perfect bibliographies amount to so much busy work and teacher brutality, you'll like the textual system. Or if you see yourself as a cautious innovator, neither wed to academic tradition nor totally disrespectful of it, the parenthetical system may offer a comfortable middle approach. In any event, check with your teacher first; he may decide for you.

What to document

You should document, in some way, all you learned during your readings that is not common knowledge. The assumption is that if you had to read to learn these things, so will other people, and they will need help getting their hands on the same materials you read. A list of the kinds of material in your text you should document resembles a list of the kinds of material you read: little-known facts and statistics, opinions of writers you cite, and all quotations and all summaries.

Sensible documentation is itself an art. You want to steer a course between too many footnotes or parenthetical references, which make your paper stuffy and labored, and too few footnotes or parenthetical references, which defeat the whole purpose of documentation—to assist the reader.

If possible, make your footnotes or parenthetical references work overtime. For instance, if a paragraph contains several pieces of information taken from the same page of the same source, one footnote or one parenthetical reference will do for all:

> Of all institutions, the military probably
> affects us most profoundly. Defense spending
> runs over 80 billion dollars a year, over a
> third of the Federal Government's budget, and
> about 10 percent of the nation's gross national
> product. National defense occupies the full-
> time efforts of some seven million civilians,
> over 10 percent of the U.S. labor force. (2:45)

Or if all the information of a paragraph was found within a few pages of a source, again one footnote or one parenthetical reference will usually do:

> Donovan, a retired Marine Corps colonel,
> feels that the war in Vietnam was the result
> of many converging vested interests--military,
> civilian, governmental--all bent on extending

```
the "scope of militarism and the activities of
the defense establishment."  Furthermore,
Donovan feels that "our military power has
come to be viewed by many people as a self-
perpetuating force of aggression and destruc-
tion motivated by many interests beyond the
needs of national defense." (2:1-3)
```

But a reference like (2:8–116) obviously serves the reader not at all. If a paragraph combines information from several widely scattered pages of the same source, separate footnotes or references will be needed: (2:8) . . . (2:67) . . . (2:116). Similarly, a paragraph that draws information from several different sources will require separate footnotes or references: (2:8) . . . (6:23) . . . (4:131). Your aim is to get by with as little documentation apparatus as possible without, of course, misleading or confusing the reader.

Formats for documentation

Over the years a number of conventions for punctuating, spacing, and ordering bibliographic information have been developed. Most of these conventions are sensible, and even the few that seem arbitrary serve at least to standardize presentations so readers know what to expect. You should practice these conventions in polishing off your paper, unless your conscience, your good sense, or your teacher suggests other approaches.

Formats for the footnoting system

Raised numbers in the text.   These usually are placed at the ends of sentences or at the ends of paragraphs. Enter the raised number after the last mark of punctuation of the sentence. If you type, enter the number a half space above the line and do not space from the last mark of punctuation of the sentence:

```
Paid admissions to movies nearly doubled
by 1929.¹
```

Footnotes and bibliographic entries.   Footnotes are placed at the bottoms of pages or gathered together in one list, headed NOTES, at the end of the paper. All footnotes at the bottom of a page are entered under an unbroken line extending from margin to margin.

In appearance, footnotes and the entries of the bibliography are nearly identical. Footnotes cite exact page numbers. Bibliographic entries for sources *published separately* (a book) show no page numbers while entries for sources *not published separately* (a magazine article) show inclusive page numbers. Footnotes show authors' names in normal order (Irving Beller) while bibliographic entries reverse first and last names (Beller, Irving).

Study the widely used formats below and note other minor differences between footnotes and bibliographic entries. ("F" means "footnote" and "B" means "bibliographic entry.")

For a book by a single author:

F   [1]John Kenneth Galbraith, The New Industrial State (Boston: Houghton Mifflin Co., 1967), p. 211.

B   Galbraith, John Kenneth. The New Industrial State. Boston: Houghton Mifflin Co., 1967.

For a book by two authors:

F   [2]Christopher Jenks and David Riesman, The Academic Revolution (New York: Doubleday & Company, Inc., 1968), p. 205.

B   Jenks, Christopher and David Riesman. The Academic Revolution. New York: Doubleday & Company, Inc., 1968.

For a book by three or more authors:

F   [3]David Riesman et al., The Lonely Crowd (Garden City, N.Y.: Doubleday Anchor Books, 1955), p. 27.

B   Riesman, David et al. The Lonely Crowd. Garden City, N.Y.: Doubleday Anchor Books, 1955.

For a book translated from a foreign language:

F   [4]Sergei Eisenstein, Film Form, trans. Jay Leyda (New York: Meridian Books, 1967), p. 258.

B   Eisenstein, Sergei. Film Form. Trans. Jay Leyda. New York: Meridian Books, 1967.

For an essay in a book of essays by different writers:

F   [5]Irving Beller, "The Concentration of Corporate Power," in Where It's At,

ed. Steven E. Deutsch and John Howard
(New York: Harper and Row, 1970), p. 93.

B   Beller, Irving. "The Concentration of
        Corporate Power." In Where It's At,
        ed. Steven E. Deutsch and John
        Howard, pp. 92-111. New York:
        Harper and Row, 1970.

For a magazine article:

F   [6]Paul Goodman, "Freedom and Learning:
The Need for Choice," The Saturday Review,
LI (May 18, 1968), 75.

B   Goodman, Paul. "Freedom and Learning:
        The Need for Choice," The Saturday
        Review, LI (May 18, 1968), 73-75.

For a newspaper story:

F   [7]David Hapgood, "The Diploma: A
Meaningless, if Powerful, Piece of Paper,"
Los Angeles Times, August 3, 1969, sec.
F, p. 1.

B   Hapgood, David. "The Diploma: A Meaning-
        less, if Powerful, Piece of Paper,"
        Los Angeles Times, August 3, 1969,
        sec. F, p. 1-2.

For an encyclopedia entry:

F   [8]Arthur Knight, "Motion Pictures,"
The World Book Encyclopedia (1970), 13,
716.

B   Knight, Arthur. "Motion Pictures," The
        World Book Encyclopedia (1970), 13,
        702-720.

For an unsigned source:

F   [9]"Jobs: Is College Needed?" The
Fresno Bee, July 5, 1970, sec. C, p. 1.

B   "Jobs: Is College Needed?" The Fresno
        Bee, July 5, 1970, sec. C, p. 1.

For an interview:

F   [10]Interview with Milton Lessinger, Professor of Cinema, University of Southern California, November 13, 1970.

B   Lessinger, Milton. Professor of Cinema, University of Southern California. Interview, November 13, 1970.

For a radio or TV program:

F   [11]"The Today Show," N.B.C. telecast, January 12, 1971.

B   "The Today Show," N.B.C. telecast, January 12, 1971.

SIMPLIFIED FORMATS FOR FOOTNOTES AND BIBLIOGRAPHIC ENTRIES. Like many conventions, the "authorized" formats listed above are based as much on reason and common sense as on blind tradition, accident, and the idiosyncrasies of a handful of experts who decide such matters. As a result, these formats, in my view, are in need of some revision and simplification. If a careful reader, you may have noticed how parentheses occur in footnotes but not in bibliographic entries, how authors' names end in commas in footnotes and in periods in bibliographic entries, how "p." and "pp." occur before page numbers of works not issued in volumes but are omitted before page numbers of works that are issued in volumes. If your teacher or department doesn't object, you might follow these guidelines and simplified formats for writing your footnotes and bibliographic entries:

1. Use periods after authors' names in both footnotes and bibliographic entries.

2. Separate other information with commas only (no colons or parentheses) in both footnotes and bibliographic entries.

3. Precede *all* page numbers, whether a single page or several pages, with "p."

4. Do not cite cities of publication of books or volume numbers of magazines—superfluous information.

Thus:

For a book by a single author:

F   [1]John Kenneth Galbraith. The New Industrial State, Houghton Mifflin Co., 1967, p. 211.

B   Galbraith, John Kenneth. <u>The</u> <u>New</u> <u>Industrial</u> <u>State</u>, Houghton Mifflin Co., 1967.

For a book by two authors:

F   [2]Christopher Jenks and David Riesman. <u>The</u> <u>Academic</u> <u>Revolution</u>, Doubleday and Company, Inc., 1968, p. 205.

B   Jenks, Christopher and David Riesman. <u>The</u> <u>Academic</u> <u>Revolution</u>, Doubleday and Company, Inc., 1968.

For a book by three or more authors:

F   [3]David Riesman and others. <u>The</u> <u>Lonely</u> <u>Crowd</u>, Doubleday Anchor Books, 1955, p. 27.

B   Riesman, David and others. <u>The</u> <u>Lonely</u> <u>Crowd</u>, Doubleday Anchor Books, 1955.

For a book translated from a foreign language:

F   [4]Sergei Eisenstein. <u>Film</u> <u>Form</u>, translated by Jay Leyda, Meridian Books, 1967, p. 258.

B   Eisenstein, Sergei. <u>Film</u> <u>Form</u>, translated by Jay Leyda, Meridian Books, 1967.

For an essay in a book of essays by different writers:

F   [5]Irving Beller. "The Concentration of Corporate Power," in <u>Where</u> <u>It's</u> <u>At</u>, edited by Steven E. Deutsch and John Howard, Harper and Row, 1970, p. 93.

B   Beller, Irving. "The Concentration of Corporate Power," in <u>Where</u> <u>It's</u> <u>At</u>, edited by Steven E. Deutsch and John Howard, Harper and Row, 1970, p. 92-111.

For a magazine article:

F   [6]Paul Goodman. "Freedom and Learning: The Need for Choice," The Saturday Review, May 18, 1968, p. 75.

B   Goodman, Paul. "Freedom and Learning: The Need for Choice," The Saturday Review, May 18, 1968, p. 73-75.

For a newspaper story:

F   [7]David Hapgood. "The Diploma: A Meaningless, if Powerful, Piece of Paper," Los Angeles Times, August 3, 1969, sec. F, p. 1.

B   Hapgood, David. "The Diploma: A Meaningless, if Powerful, Piece of Paper," Los Angeles Times, August 3, 1969, sec. F, p. 1-2.

For an encyclopedia entry:

F   [8]Arthur Knight. "Motion Pictures," The World Book Encyclopedia, 1970, vol. 13, p. 716.

B   Knight, Arthur. "Motion Pictures," The World Book Encyclopedia, 1970, vol. 13, p. 702-720.

For an unsigned source:

F   [9]"Jobs: Is College Needed?" The Fresno Bee, July 5, 1970, sec. C, p. 1.

B   "Jobs: Is College Needed?" The Fresno Bee, July 5, 1970, sec. C, p. 1.

For an interview:

F   [10]Interview with Milton Lessinger, Professor of Cinema, University of Southern California, November 13, 1970.

B   Lessinger, Milton. Professor of Cinema, University of Southern California, interview, November 13, 1970.

For a radio or TV program:

F   [11]"The Today Show." N.B.C. telecast,
January 12, 1971.

B   "The Today Show." N.B.C. telecast,
        January 12, 1971.

These models should take care of the different kinds of materials your paper might use. If they don't, develop your own formats from the formats listed above. Formats for poems and stories in books may be treated similarly to the format for an essay in a collection of essays. Pamphlets may be regarded as books. Reference works may be set up in the format of a book or an encyclopedia entry.

Multiple footnotes for the same source. If you have more than one footnote for the same source (same book or article), only the first footnote needs to be complete. Subsequent footnotes need to show only the author's last name and the page number:

[1]Arthur Knight. The Liveliest Art,
Mentor Books, 1957, p. 147.

[2]Knight, p. 145-46.

[3]Knight, p. 142.

If you have more than one source by the same author, and if you have several footnotes for these sources, subsequent footnotes will have to include titles to avoid confusion:

[1]Arthur Knight. The Liveliest Art,
Mentor Books, 1957, p. 147.

[2]Arthur Knight. "Motion Pictures," The
World Book Encyclopedia, 1970, vol. 13, p. 716.

[3]Knight, The Liveliest Art, p. 145-46.

[4]Knight, "Motion Pictures," p. 707.

Sample bibliography for footnoting system. Note how entries are alphabetized. Entries running over one line are single spaced, and all lines after the first are indented five spaces.

BIBLIOGRAPHY

Bazin, Andre. "The Evolution of the Language
    of Cinema," in Film and the Liberal Arts,
    edited by T. J. Ross, Holt, Rinehart and
    Winston, Inc., p. 8-13.

Eisenstein, Sergei. _Film Form_, translated by
    Jay Leyda, Meridian Books, 1967.

Eisenstein, Sergei and others. "A Statement,"
    in _Film Form_, by Sergei Eisenstein,
    translated by Jay Leyda, Meridian Books,
    1967, p. 257-60.

Knight, Arthur. _The Liveliest Art_, Mentor
    Books, 1957.

McLuhan, Marshall. _Understanding Media_,
    Mentor Books, 1964.

Montagu, Ivor. _Film World_, Penguin Books,
    1967.

Spottiswoode, Raymond. _A Grammar of the Film_,
    University of California Press, 1965.

Formats for the parenthetical reference system

Parenthetical references.   Like raised numbers for the footnoting system, parenthetical references are placed at the ends of sentences, after all marks of punctuation, or at the ends of paragraphs. If you type, single space from the last mark of punctuation of the preceding sentence, and double space to the next sentence.

Over two thousand institutions of higher
learning employ half a million people and hold
about seven million students. (10:2) But
this is only part of the story.

(In this example, the 10 refers to the tenth source of the bibliography and the 2 refers to page 2.)

Sample bibliography for the parenthetical reference system.
The format of the bibliography for the parenthetical reference system is identical to that of the footnoting system (see pages 123 and 124) _except that the entries have been numbered consecutively:_

BIBLIOGRAPHY

1.   Beller, Irving. "The Concentration of
        Corporate Power," in _Where It's At_,
        edited by Steven E. Deutsch and
        John Howard, Harper and Row, 1970,
        p. 92-111.

2. Berg, Ivar. _Education_ and _Jobs_: _The_
    Great _Training_ _Robbery_, Praeger
    Publishers, 1970.

3. Donovan, Colonel James A. _Militarism_,
    _U.S.A._, Charles Scribner's Sons,
    1970.

4. Galbraith, John Kenneth. _The_ _New_ _Indus-_
    trial _State_, Houghton Mifflin Co.,
    1967.

5. Goodman, Paul. "Freedom and Learning:
    The Need for Choice," _The_ _Saturday_
    Review, May 18, 1968, p. 73-75.

6. Hapgood, David. "The Diploma: A Meaning-
    less, if Powerful, Piece of Paper,"
    Los _Angeles_ _Times_, August 3, 1969,
    sec. F, p. 1-2.

7. Illich, Ivan. "Schooling: The Ritual of
    Progress," _The_ _New_ _York_ _Review_,
    December 3, 1970, p. 20-26.

8. Illich, Ivan. "Why We Must Abolish
    Schooling," _The_ _New_ _York_ _Review_,
    July 2, 1970, p. 9-14.

9. Jenks, Christopher and David Riesman.
    The _Academic_ _Revolution_, Doubleday
    & Company, Inc., 1968.

10. "Jobs: Is College Needed?" _The_ _Fresno_
    Bee, July 5, 1970, sec. C, p. 1.

11. Mills, C. Wright. "The Structure of Power
    in American Society," in _Where_ _It's_
    _At_, edited by Steven E. Deutsch and
    John Howard, Harper and Row, 1970,
    p. 83-91.

12. Ridgeway, James. _The_ _Closed_ _Corporation_,
    Ballantine Books, 1969.

13. Sexton, Patricia Cayo. _The_ _American_
    School, Prentice-Hall, 1967.

14. Trombley, William. "UC Facing Most Basic Changes in Its History," <u>Los Angeles Times</u>, February 1, 1971, sec. II, p. 1-2.

Final reminder: Since individual colleges, departments, and teachers sometimes prefer certain formats over others, you should always make inquiries about these matters before adopting any particular system of formats.

Formats for textual documentation If you have occasion to mention the titles of your sources in your running text, follow these guidelines:

1. Titles of sources *published separately* are underlined with key words capitalized:

> *a book:* <u>Film Form</u>
> *name of newspaper:* <u>Los Angeles Times</u>
> *name of magazine:* <u>The Saturday Review</u>

2. Titles of sources *not published separately* are set in quotation marks with key words capitalized:

> *a magazine article:* "Freedom and Learning: The Need for Choice"
> *a newspaper story:* "Jobs: Is College Needed?"
> *an essay, poem, or story from a book:* "The Concentration of Corporate Power"

If you wish to insert page numbers *in your text* (instead of using footnotes to show page numbers) insert these wherever you would have used raised numbers or parenthetical references. Enclose page numbers in parentheses and precede with "p.":

In his book <u>The Liveliest Art</u>, film historian Arthur Knight has pointed out that paid attendance at movies nearly doubled in the three years following the release of <u>The Jazz Singer</u>, the first feature-length movie to use the new sound system. (p. 142)

Formats for quoted material

Longer quotations If the passage you are quoting is rather lengthy and threatens to run over four lines of your text, you should set it off by single spacing the passage and indenting an extra five spaces from both margins. These longer quotations need no quotation marks since the solid, set-off look of the passage tells your reader you are quoting.

Punctuation with close quotation mark   This gives students all sorts of trouble when it needn't. A very simple rule governs the placement of punctuation marks that occur at the ends of quotations: Periods and commas go *inside* the last quotation mark while colons and semicolons go *outside.* Examples:

Period with close quotation mark:

Eisenstein and his colleagues felt that "only a contrapuntal use of sound in relation to the visual montage will afford a new potentiality of montage development and perfection."

<small>**Eisenstein's period**</small>

Eisenstein felt that film art could be enhanced through "a contrapuntal use of sound."

<small>**student's period**</small>

Comma with close quotation mark:

Eisenstein felt that "a contrapuntal use of sound," which he and his colleagues proposed in 1928, could enhance film art.

Colon with close quotation mark:

Eisenstein felt that film art might be enhanced through "a contrapuntal use of sound": the unexpected pairing of a sound and an image.

Semicolon with close quotation mark:

Eisenstein felt that film art might be enhanced through "a contrapuntal use of sound"; later filmmakers apparently developed similar theories, though largely unaware of Eisenstein's proposal.

The placement of the question mark with the close quotation mark depends on whether the question mark was introduced by you or the writer you are quoting. If you end your own question with a quotation, place your question mark *outside* the close quotation mark:

What did Eisenstein mean by "a contrapuntal use of sound"?

But if the original passage contained a question mark, place it *inside* the close quotation mark:

Ivor Montagu asks: "What should be...the relation of picture and sound?"

The same rule applies to the placement of the close parenthesis: If yours, place it *outside* the close quotation mark:

Eisenstein wanted to explore the possibilities of sound (e.g., its "contrapuntal use") for enhancing film art.

If the writer's, place it *inside:*

Montagu has suggested that if sound and image are connected by context rather than by chance, "they will be no more confusing than counterpoint in music (which [are] two different things, connected by context, both auditory)."

Italicized quotations If the passage you are quoting contains italicized words or phrases for stress or emphasis, you should be faithful to the original by underlining those same words or phrases in your paper. If you wish to stress portions of the original that are not italicized, you may underline certain key words, phrases, or even a whole sentence or two. But then the reader will not know who stressed the material, you or the author. To clarify matters it is customary to bracket in a brief note at the end of a quotation in which italics appear to explain who added the stress. Use [stress in original] for quotations with underlined word representing italics in the original; use [stress added] for quotations containing words that you underlined for stress. Examples:

Italics appeared in original passage:

"School is a ritual of initiation which introduces the neophyte to the sacred rite of progressive consumption, a ritual of propitiation whose academic priests mediate between the faithful and the gods of privilege and power, a ritual of expiation which sacrifices its dropouts, branding them as scapegoats of underdevelopment." [stress in original]

Stress added by writer:

"The distinctions that many Americans do not make is this: Jobs in the future may require more schooling than in the past, but that schooling does not necessarily mean more college education." [stress added]

Quoting quoted material   Occasionally, the material you choose to quote will itself contain words, phrases, or sentences surrounded by quotation marks the author added. Set this material off with *single* (rather than double) quotation marks:

Original passage:

```
Is the present popular attitude that "everyone
is entitled to a college education" really
needed?
```

The passage quoted:

```
Associated Press asks, "Is the present popular
attitude that 'everyone is entitled to a
college education' really needed?"
```

Typewritten format

Typewritten manuscripts are double spaced with margins set an inch from the left and right edges of the paper. If your teacher requires a cover, leave an inch and a half margin at the left of your text to allow for punching holes to fix the pages in the cover. As you type, leave an inch margin at the top and bottom. Always use a black ribbon, and plan, too, to replace the ribbon every so often.

Make all your corrections by erasing. Use easy-erase paper if you like, but don't put your elbows on freshly typed sheets. They smear easily. Don't use onion skin or extra-thin paper. Your teacher's red ball point rips right through it, even when he's not mad at you. Plan to make a carbon copy. Many instructors prefer not to return term papers so students can't sell them next year. If you are an uncertain typist, or if your girl is busy near the due date, give yourself (or her) enough time to type your paper leisurely to avoid the wholesale errors in spelling, omissions, and repetitions that seem to plague typists about three in the morning.

Contents   If you use a cover, pick a color appropriate to your subject: apocalyptic black or grey for subjects like pollution, cancer, and the bomb; bold yellow or flippant orange for subjects like sex, rock, drugs, hippies, and the Age of Aquarius. Into the cover should go, in this order:

The title page.   One-third down from the top margin enter the title of your paper, centered and in upper case (capital letters). Do not draw lines under the title or set it in quotation marks. Half way down the title page, enter your name, centered and in lower case, like this:

```
                    by
              Joanie Wonder
```

One-third from the bottom of the title page, centered and in lower case, something like this:

```
English 1A
Mr. Iverson
12:00 MWF
May 17, 1972
```

A few funny students still want to include somewhere, "submitted in partial fulfillment of the requirements of English 1A." Don't you be tempted.

The text. Begin your first page about a fourth of the way down from the top. Repeat your title, again centered and in upper case. Do not draw lines under the title or set it in quotation marks. Do not repeat your name. Drop down four spaces and begin typing your paper.

You may wish to break up the text into sections or "chapterettes." These will probably correspond to the major headings of your outline. You may title these sections or you may simply use numbers to head them. If you title the section, center the title, underline it, and put it in lower case with key words capitalized:

<u>Early Efforts to Stop Water Pollution</u>

Don't start a fresh page for a new section; simply triple space to the section title or number and triple space again from the section title to the first line of the new section. If you wish to further divide the section, run the title of the subsection against the left margin and triple space to the next line.

The first page of your text is usually not numbered, but all subsequent pages are. Enter page numbers either at the bottoms of pages, centered, or in the upper righthand corners. No periods, dashes, or understrokes. Any material placed *before* the title page —a note, an outline, a dedication to your mother, a snappy quotation—should be numbered with Roman numerals in lower case.

The bibliography. This is a list of the sources you used. It will conclude your paper. If you have a minimum page requirement to meet, the bibliography does not usually count toward the requirement, nor does the title page. (For the format of the bibliography, see pages 118-26.)

Other material. Charts, graphs, tables, photographs, and like material may be interspersed in the text where appropriate or gathered into an appendix before the bibliography. This material doesn't count toward a minimum page requirement either. Outlines may serve as tables of contents. If you decide to include one with your paper, place it after the title page and before the first page of text. Head your outline with your thesis sentence and try to compose all entries as complete sentences. Single space all entries that run over one line, and double space between entries.

AFTERCHAPTER

The Longer Paper

Finish off your paper by documenting your sources. Double-check the format of your footnotes and/or bibliography for completeness and consistency. Also check the format of your quoted material, including end punctuation, for correctness. Whether you write your paper in ink or type it, follow the suggested format that closes this chapter.

Activities

1. Put the following sources into proper formats for both footnotes and bibliographic entries. Use either the standard or simplified formats, but stick to one or the other. Examples using standard formats:
   a book: title: Outer Space; author: James P. Orm; information from page 31; publisher: Random House; city of publication: New York; year of publication: 1971.
   Footnote:

   ¹James P. Orm, <u>Outer Space</u> (New York: Random House, 1971), p. 31.

   Bibliographic entry:
   Orm, James P. <u>Outer Space.</u> New York: Random House, 1971.

   A. *A book:* title: Mars and Beyond; author: Edgar Clemson and J. P. House; information from pages 3 and 4; publisher: Houghton Mifflin Co.; city of publication: Boston, year of publication: 1968.
   B. *An essay from a book of essays by different writers:* title of essay: Manned Satellites; title of book: On the Frontiers of Space; author of essay: Hamilton Smith; editor of book: Jason Wundt; inclusive pages of essay: 149-168; information from page 151; publisher: Prentice-Hall; city of publication: Englewood Cliffs, N.J.; year of publication: 1969.
   C. *A magazine article:* title of article: Funding the Mars Project; name of magazine: The Journal of Old Priorities; author: Joseph Sear Sage; inclusive pages of article: 63-66; information from page 63; volume number of magazine: XXVI; date of magazine: March 16, 1971.
   D. *A newspaper story:* Headline: Congress Slashes Space Funding; reporter: unknown; name of newspaper: The Washington Post; section: A; information taken from page 1; inclusive pages of story: 1, 13; date of story: June 4, 1971.
   E. *A reference work:* title of entry: Space; name of contributor: George P. Wilson; title of work: The World Book Encyclopedia;

volume number: 19; information taken from page 451; inclusive pages of entry: 449-456; year of publication: 1970.

2. Explain:
   A. The format for longer quotations.
   B. The placement of the comma, period, semicolon, colon, question mark, and parentheses with close quotation mark.
   C. The purpose of [stress in original] and [stress added].
   D. The format for quoting quoted material.

IV
SAMPLES

They had become the richest people on the globe; would they use their wealth to prosper society or to display power? They were democratic in law; would they be democratic in fact? They had developed technology to its highest point; would they learn to make technology their servant rather than their master? They were using up their resources more rapidly than they were replacing them; would science reverse the process, or would they be forced to a lower standard of living or to economic imperialism?

—*Henry Steele Commager*

The new sensibility—*baby baby baby where did our love go?*—the new world, submerged so long, invisible, and now arising, slippy, shiny, electric —Super-Scuba man!—out of the vinyl deeps.

—*Tom Wolfe*

10
The Longer Paper

Much of the illustrative material in previous chapters has been collected in this chapter to take shape as two longer papers, one about the art of motion pictures, the other dealing with the institutional deficiencies of colleges.

I wrote both papers.[1] They represent answers to questions that have interested me. I tried to write these papers to contrast with each other and to illustrate two approaches to independent study. The first paper on film represents a relatively undeflected line of inquiry from research question to thesis; from

> What impact did the advent of sound in 1927 have on the later development of film art?

to

> The advent of sound in 1927 at first posed a threat to the developing art of cinema, and only gradually won a place in the repertoire of editing principles established during the silent era.

The second paper on colleges followed a rather roundabout journey, with many side trips into topics I later found to be relevant; from

> What is the connection between the so-called military-industrial complex and our system of college education?

to

> Like other overgrown institutions, our system of college education has become self-serving and wasteful, and its influence should now be restricted to allow alternatives to flourish.

The paper on colleges, then, is purposely more far-ranging, purposely broader than the film paper, although I believe it has unity and direction. If my readings for this paper lacked depth, I hoped to make up in breadth, perspective, and relatedness. The paper on colleges also represents an attempt to combine several of the strate-

---

[1]Just as I wrote all the illustrative material in this section of the book—to see if I can follow my own advice.

gies for researching a topic and writing about it explained in Chapter 2. The dominant strategy is problem and solution, but the strategies of deduction, cause and effect, comparison, and itemization also appear in the paper. The first kind of paper, the film paper, tends to produce a specialist; the second kind of paper produces a generalist. Who can say which researcher benefits more from his efforts?

The first paper follows a simplified format for footnoting, while the second paper uses parenthetical references for documentation (see Chapter 9). Both papers include marginal notes keyed to material in earlier chapters.

Typewritten
format,
p. 129-31.

SOUND AND THE ART OF FILM

The advent of the optical sound track in the late 1920s was probably the single most important technical development for advancing the art of film since 1889 when George Eastman finally succeeded in coating strips of celluloid with photographic emulsion. Before sound, of course, filmmakers had to say everything in pictures; with sound the filmmaker's options were increased considerably. And no technical breakthrough since sound — color, wide screen, stereoptic photography — has had quite the same impact. But what many modern moviegoers don't realize, perhaps, is that the advent of sound was not exactly welcomed by most serious filmmakers of the time. In fact, sound at first actually posed a threat to the developing art of cinema, and only gradually won a place in the repertoire of editing principles first established during the silent-film era.

Intro-
duction,
p. 97-98.

Thesis,
p. 11-12,
67-70.

I

Filmmakers have always been interested in the technical aspects of their art, but the introduction of sound in 1927 seems to have

Back-
ground,
p. 98-99.

been the brainchild of the businessmen who ran the great Hollywood studios. According to Arthur Knight, sound was added to movies as a gimmick to shore up the industry's sagging box office. It worked. Paid admissions nearly doubled by 1929 and as Knight puts it, "The panic was on."[1]

Background, p. 98-99.

The sound system introduced in 1927 with Warner Brother's The Jazz Singer, and still used today, wedded picture and sound on the same strip of film, making perfect synchronization possible. Not only could the series of images be spliced to get the best shots in the right length and order, but the accompanying sound too could be edited for maximum effect.

Paragraph of summary, p. 57-58.

Moviemakers no longer had to rely solely on a flow of pictures to tell their stories, and the often clumsy device of the title for advancing the story could at last be replaced by the spoken word.[2]

Note lead-ins to quotations, p. 105-6.

But the silent film was in no way a primitive, half-realized art form. Knight describes the best silent films as having "created a world of persuasive reality despite the absence of voices and the verifying clangor of natural sound."[3] The art of silent film was mainly the art of editing. The purpose of film editing, then as now, is to arrange separate shots in such a way as to produce a total effect. For film critic Ivor Montagu, the development of film editing was "the discovery that shots rightly selected and viewed from

Tagline: "film critic," p. 106-7.

Footnote, p. 120-23.

[1]Arthur Knight. The Liveliest Art, Mentor Books, 1957, p. 147.

[2]Knight, p. 145-46.

the correct angle, in a right order, cut to the right length, beginning and ending at the right moment are apprehended as a single whole." [stress in original][4]

Stress in original, p. 128.

Knight credits the American silent-era director D. W. Griffith with developing most of the editing principles still in use today. It was Griffith who first understood that scenes could be presented from different ranges and angles, something the stage play could never do. Griffith also discovered that much unimportant action could be cut to tighten the stream of events, just as the length of many shots could be shortened or lengthened to affect mood and tempo. Finally, Griffith also developed the technique of cross-cutting, or advancing two or more lines of action at the same time. All of these techniques helped film find an identity apart from the stage play.[5]

Para-graphing, p. 99-102.

During the 1920s, Russian filmmakers experimented extensively with the basic principles Griffith developed. Lev Kuleshov, for instance, obtained close-up footage of an expressionless male actor. To this footage he spliced first a shot of a bowl of soup, then a shot of a child playing with a stuffed animal, and finally a dead woman in a coffin. Audiences to whom the spliced footage was shown raved about the actor's performance. Never had they

---

[3]Knight, p. 142.

[4]Ivor Montagu. *Film World*, Penguin Books, 1964, p. 109.

[5]Knight, p. 32.

Subsequent footnotes, same source, p. 123.

seen such an expression of hunger, such
fatherly affection, such grief. As Knight
explains, "it is not merely the image alone,
but the juxtaposition of images that creates
the emotional tone of a sequence."[6]

Kuleshov's colleague, Sergei Eisenstein,
wrote about the editing principle, or what he
called "montage." Eisenstein based his theories
on the Japanese ideogram or picture-symbol.
Ideograms unite at least two concepts to form a
third concept. For instance, the Japanese
ideogram for weeping joins a picture for water
and a picture for eye. Film art, according to
Eisenstein, is derived from similar unions.[7]
Andre Bazin feels that editing of this type
alludes rather than shows: "none of the concrete elements ... are to be found in the
[Brackets], premises; [a shot of] maidens plus [a shot of]
p. 104-5. appletrees in bloom equal hope."[8]

However, not all filmmakers agreed with
Eisenstein, as Montagu suggests:

Longer
quotation,
p. 126.

> Pudovkin [another Russian filmmaker] said that
> the joining together of two shots by editing
> partook of the nature of a sum (a + b).
> Eisenstein denied it. The result, he insisted,
> is neither the sum nor the product (ab) but a
> totally new term (c).[9]

---

[6]Knight, p. 72-73.

[7]Sergei Eisenstein, _Film Form_, translated
by Jay Leyda, Meridian Books, 1967, p. 29-30.

[8]Andre Bazin. "The Evolution of the
Language of Cinema," in _Film and the Liberal
Arts_, edited by T. J. Ross, Holt, Rinehart
and Winston, 1970, p. 10.

[9]Montagu, p. 121.

In any case, filmmakers like Griffith and Eisenstein, along with numerous other film-makers in Germany, France, Scandanavia, and England, succeeded in developing a unique visual art form. There were, to be sure, many silent movies whose sole purpose was to make money for their backers. But film historians like Knight make it clear that the silent era produced many authentic master-pieces to which sound would have added nothing.

Connecting ideas: "in any case," "to be sure," "but," p. 110.

II

New section, p. 130.

If anything, sound, when it first ap-peared, threatened to inhibit further develop-ment of the cinematic art. As Raymond Spottiswoode has pointed out, before 1928 film was an international art form. Since movies used no spoken dialogue, the nationalities of the actors mattered not at all. It was a simple procedure to edit in titles written in the language of whatever country a film played in. But sound changed all this. If film-makers hoped to maintain an international market for their products, they had to shoot the same script several times in different languages. According to Spottiswoode, "inspiration was crushed by the sheer weight of repetition."[10] Soon filmmakers abandoned multilingual productions; the cinema became nationalized and the flow of new filmic ideas among countries was inhibited.

The earliest talkies also tended to resemble stage plays, much as the earliest,

---

[10]Raymond Spottiswoode. A Grammar of the Film, The University of California Press, 1965, p. 75.

crudely produced silent films imitated live
theatre before Griffith gave film an identity
of its own. In fact, because original scripts
for talkies were scarce, the first sound
movies, according to Knight, amounted to little
more than "static, photographed stage plays...

Quoting
quoted
material,
p. 129.
'all-talking, all-singing' musicals in which
raw sound was exploited in every imaginable
way."[11]

The public wanted sound, lots of it, and
Hollywood obliged. The new breed of movie
actors produced by sound talked constantly.
And if the public wanted to hear words, it also
wanted a lot of sound effects: doors slamming,
cars crashing, sirens wailing, tap dancers
tapping, and trumpets trumpeting. The rush to
sound meant that the source of every sound had
to be seen and every object shown that could
conceivably make a noise did. No sound
apparently was too banal to delight moviegoers.
Knight describes how Mack Sennet's comedy The
Family Picnic "regaled [audiences] by the
sounds of the picnickers crunching celery or
munching potato chips."[12]

The camera, too, once mobile, now had to
be enclosed in a soundproof box so the sound
of its whirling gears would not be picked up
by the microphone. Scenes could no longer be
shot from changing ranges and angles.
Visually, "The resulting films," writes
Montagu, "were truly dull."[13] It was almost

---

[11]Knight, p. 148.

[12]Knight, p. 148.

[13]Montagu, p. 151.

as if film art had retreated to pre-Griffith days. Knight laments, "In no time at all the techniques, the artistry that directors had acquired through the years of silent films were cast aside and forgotten in the shadow of the microphone."[14]

Note lead-ins to quotations, p. 105-6.

III

In the late twenties, Eisenstein, along with his fellow filmmakers V. I. Pudovkin and G. V. Alexandrov, issued a statement on the future use of sound in films. The three, while recognizing that sound was here to stay, warned that its overuse could "hinder the development and perfection of cinema as an art [while it] threatens to destroy all its present formal achievements."[15] These Russians proposed that sound be used "contrapuntally" and "nonsynchronically."[16] This means that sound and image need not always be "naturally" related; instead filmmakers might explore the possibilities of new sound-image montages. Sound and image should combine to produce a third, greater effect.

Unfortunately, the Russians' brief statement offers no examples of how sound might be joined contrapuntally or non-synchronically with image. But Montagu has

Connecting ideas: "Unfortu-nately," "but,"

---

[14]Knight, p. 148.

[15]Sergei Eisenstein and others. "A Statement," in Film Form by Sergei Eisenstein, translated by Jay Leyda, Meridian Books, 1967, p. 257.

[16]Eisenstein, "A Statement," p. 258.

"instead,"
"for
instance,"
"thus,"
p. 110.

enlarged on the Russians' theories. Non-synchronization, Montagu explains, means that the source of sounds need not always be shown. Instead, the screen should show something else more meaningful as a sound is heard. What is important is not to show the source of the sound, but what it means. For instance, a man who expects to be killed hears approaching footsteps. The screen shows not the feet of the killer but the expression on the face of the victim. Thus image (the victim's face) and sound (the footsteps) combine to produce a third effect: impending death.[17]

Montagu describes how Eisenstein used sound contrapuntally in his Ivan the Terrible. Visually, the film is slow-paced, but the dialogue moves fast. As characters speak the camera fixes on other characters and objects so that "the sound acts as a rhythmic counterpoint link to the jump-rhythm of the images succeeding each other."[18]

Montagu doubts that manifestos such as that issued by Eisenstein, Pudovkin, and Alexandrov had much direct effect on the future course of film art.[19] In any event, later filmmakers gradually solved the technical problems sound posed and learned to use sound in ways anticipated by the Russians. Knight explains, for instance, how the process of postdubbing allowed cameramen to emerge from their soundproof booths and rediscover the

---

[17]Montagu, p. 162.

[18]Montagu, p. 161.

[19]Montagu, p. 153.

possibilities of the mobile camera. Later on, Knight explains, the mechanism of the camera itself was soundproofed.[20]

Knight feels that the director Ernst Lubitsch, a German imported by Paramount Studios, was among the first to discover (or to convince movie executives) that movies didn't have to talk all the time or reproduce every sound suggested by pictures. In his Love Parade and Monte Carlo, Lubitsch filmed many scenes without dialogue or sound. His audiences were, as Knight puts it, "delighted to find a new element in the talkies — silence!"[21]

The French director Rene Clair also used sound sparingly. In Sous les Troits, Clair used sound nonsynchronically to heighten the effect of a fistfight, enacted to the sound of a rushing locomotive. Audiences saw the fight taking place near a railroad track, but they heard the locomotive rather than the sounds of the fight. The intensity of the locomotive suggested the fury of the fighters more effectively than sounds of blows and groans would have.[22]

In his 39 Steps, Alfred Hitchcock blended the scream of a woman, which concluded one scene, with the whistle of a locomotive, which began the next scene.[23] In this instance,

---

[20]Knight, p. 153.

[21]Knight, p. 151.

[22]Knight, p. 155.

[23]Knight, p. 168

different though similar sounds were used as a means of transition. Thus in addition to the image-to-image and sound-to-image editing principles advanced by theorists like Eisenstein, the possibilities of sound-to-sound montage were introduced. The repertoire of film editing principles was now complete, though still not fully explored.

My readings suggested that film theorists are not in agreement about the relationship of sound to image. Montagu, for instance, still feels that film is basically a visual medium:

Ellipsis marks: (...), p. 103-4.

...picture is primary. The problem is to find the sound to go with the picture, rather than the picture to go with the sound. This is not because the picture is "better" in some indefinite way than sound. But simply because sound is sound and movies are pictures.[24]

Spottiswoode, on the other hand, seems prepared to promote sound to a status equal to image. For him, "The Total Film" comprises both a visual and aural factor, and neither is more "basic" than the other.[25] Marshall McLuhan insists that the union of sound and image has, after all, produced a new form of communication:

Ellipsis marks: (...), p. 103-4.

The hybrid or the meeting of two media is a moment of truth and revelation from which new form is born...a moment of freedom and release from the ordinary trance and numbness imposed by them on our senses.[26]

---

[24]Montagu, p. 153.

[25]Spottiswoode, p. 26.

[26]Marshall McLuhan. <u>Understanding Media</u>, Mentor Books, 1964, p. 63.

Bazin believes that silent film, though eminently artful, could never do more than suggest or evoke; but sound allows filmmakers to _write_ in film and become, "at last, the equal of the novelist."[27]

For my part, the sound film is not fundamentally different from the silent film: Both draw their power from the juxtaposition of dissimilar elements, whether sound or images. The history of cinema, before and after sound, is the story of discovering the right combination of elements to produce the right effect.

> **Writer's opinion identified, p. 107.**
>
> **Conclusion, p. 102.**

BIBLIOGRAPHY

Bazin, Andre. "The Evolution of the Language of Cinema," in _Film and The Liberal Arts_, edited by T. J. Ross, Holt, Rinehart and Winston, Inc., p. 8-13.

Eisenstein, Sergei. _Film Form_, translated by Jay Leyda, Meridian Books, 1967.

Eisenstein, Sergei and others. "A Statement," in _Film Form_, by Sergei Eisenstein, translated by Jay Leyda, Meridian Books, 1967, p. 257-60.

Knight, Arthur. _The Liveliest Art_, Mentor Books, 1957.

McLuhan, Marshall. _Understanding Media_, Mentor Books, 1964.

Montagu, Ivor. _Film World_, Penguin Books, 1967.

Spottiswoode, Raymond. _A Grammar of the Film_, University of California Press, 1965.

> **Bibliography, p. 120-24.**

---

[27]Bazin, p. 13.

AFTER THE WAR: ALTERNATIVES
TO COLLEGE

Intro-
duction,
p. 97-98.
Before Vietnam, the institution of the military commanded the deep respect of nearly all Americans. A large military was not only thought to be necessary, it was a patriotic duty. A large military, it was believed, kept the peace around the world and preserved America's freedom against the designs of potential aggressors. But since Vietnam, both the prestige and the credibility of the military have unquestionably suffered. Many Americans now wonder if the military has to be so large. They suspect they have been oversold on the threat of world communism, and they want to scale down the military to divert money to more pressing domestic problems. Furthermore, an increasing number of Americans fear that the military's influence will grow still more, not to meet real threats to the nation's security, but to serve various defense-related interest groups.

Intro-
duction
con-
cluded.
But if Vietnam has revealed how wasteful and self-serving the institution of the military has become, the same lesson might apply to other large institutions that affect the lives of most Americans--big government, big business, big labor, big medicine, and big education. How many of these institutions, if each had a Vietnam to expose it, would be revealed to be equally as insensitive to the public interest as the military apparently is? There is evidence, I believe, to show that our system of college education must be listed among those large institutions in need of basic reform. Like other overgrown institutions, our college system has become self-serving and wasteful, and in my opinion its influence

should now be restricted to allow alternatives to flourish.

Thesis, p. 15-16, 67-70.

The Institutional Setting

The growth of our college system, and its effects on the nation, might be better understood if related to the growth of other large institutions that have come to dominate our lives, especially since World War II. The sociologist C. Wright Mills was an early critic of large institutions. In 1957 Mills proposed that a "power elite," consisting of big government, big military, and big business working together, had emerged to affect all the "great decisions" of war and peace, prosperity and slump. (11:83) Mills insisted that the power elite operated beyond the control of the citizenry and of "middle-level" interest groups such as small businesses, labor unions, farmers' organizations, local governments, and tax payers' groups. (11:86-87) Developments since 1957 seem to have confirmed Mill's theory of a top-heavy combine of institutions that enjoy tremendous power. Irving Beller, for instance, has noted how industrial corporations, including very large ones, are merging now at a much faster rate than in the past. The concentration of economic power, according to Beller, affects all of us:

This section amounts to a first premise of a deductive strategy: "Large institutions often become self-serving and wasteful," p. 14-15.

Parenthetical reference: (11:86-87) p. 114, 124.

> The giants of American industry have tremendous wealth and there are few restrictions on how they spend it. As a result, they have been able to set cultural standards and shape the social and political, as well as the economic, forms of American society to a far greater extent than most Americans realize. They not only determine the prices we pay and the quality of the products we buy. They have an enormous influence as well...over what we buy,

Longer quotation, p. 126.

the kind of work we do, the kind of education offered our children [and] the social goals we set... . (1:93)

The economist John Kenneth Galbraith feels the nation has embarked on a new economic era which he calls "the new industrial state." According to Galbraith, the older system was Tagline:
"economist
John
Kenneth
Galbraith,"
p. 106-07. made up of corporations that sought independence from government control and operated in a market more or less sensitive to consumers' demands. The newer system, dominated by super corporations, depends heavily on the government for subsidies and other favors, and in fact has entered into a kind of partnership with government to merge industrial and state goals, especially in aerospace and defense. (4:297) Also, the newer system has so perfected the science of marketing as to minimize risk. "Consumer sovereignty" no longer applies, Galbraith maintains. The "normal sequence"-- the consumer and his demands molding the
corporation--has been reversed; now the corporation molds the consumer: "...the producing firm reaches forward to control its markets and on beyond to manage the market behavior and shape the social attitudes of those, ostensibly, that it serves." (4:212)

But of all institutions, the military probably affects us most profoundly. Defense spending now runs over 80 billion dollars a year, over a third of the federal government's budget, and about 10 percent of the nation's
Gross National Product. (3:45) National defense occupies the full-time efforts of some seven million civilians, over 10 percent of the U.S. labor force. (3:49) Clearly, defense is our biggest industry.

The defense "team," as Mills noted, is a triangle of interlocking institutions, commonly

referred to as the military-industrial complex.
Of this complex, James A. Donovan writes:

> America has become a militaristic and aggres-
> sive nation embodied in a vast, expansive, and
> burgeoning military-industrial-scientific-
> political combine which dominates the country
> and affects much of our daily life, our
> economy, our international status, and our
> foreign policies. (3:1)

Donovan, a retired Marine Corps colonel,
feels that the war in Vietnam was the result
of many converging vested interests--military,
civilian, governmental--all bent on extending
the "scope of militarism and the activities of
the defense establishment." Furthermore,
Donovan feels that "our military power has come
to be viewed by many people as a self-
perpetuating force of aggression and destruction
motivated by many interests beyond the needs
of national defense." (3:3)

Tagline: "a
retired
Marine
Corps
colonel,"
p. 106-07.

The war in Vietnam took, of course, the
lives of tens of thousands of Americans and
cost taxpayers many billions of dollars. But
the war economy has been wasteful in other
ways that have been less well publicized. Contracted research projects terminated by the
government for various reasons have already
cost taxpayers $9 billion. And a study con-
ducted by the Department of Defense itself
revealed that contractors with the poorest
efficiency records regularly received the
highest profits. (3:49-50)

Study,
p. 51.

What are the chances that Americans will
scale down their military and make its operations more sensible and economical? Not good,
according to Donovan. He writes: "This [the
spread of militarism] is happening not as a
result of a deliberate choice by the American
people, but as a result of an accumulation of

[Brackets],
p. 104-05.

military decisions, commitments, and actions that are beyond the control of present democratic processes." (3:1)

Conclusion to section, which also defines the overall problem, p. 12-13. Whatever "it" is — a power elite, an industrial state, a military-industrial complex — it seems to roll along of its own momentum, producing more agencies of government than we need, more cars and fumes than our highways and lungs can safely accommodate, more wars, weapons, and casualties than our consciences should tolerate. It appears then that many of our largest institutions serve the public not at all; rather the public serves them.

Institutional Deficiencies of Colleges

Statistics and inference, p. 47, 50-51. Many of our leading universities have apparently become willing partners of the military-industrial complex. James Ridgeway, a journalist with much experience in political reporting, found that two-thirds of all research contracted by the nation's best-known universities is connected with war and defense matters. (12:5) In addition, the federal government channels millions of dollars to "nonprofit" defense-related research centers, half of which are satellites of universities. For Cause-effect relationship, p. 11-12. Ridgeway all this means that "the major universities have become first captive and then active advocates for the military and para-military agencies of government in order to get more money for research." (12:6)

Ridgeway maintains that the modern university exists primarily to carry out war-related research and to provide professors launching pads to orbit their own careers in advising industry. Learning and job training in the traditional sense are not prominent in Ridgeway's portrait. Undergraduates lie in "holding pens" and are useful primarily for financing the university. Graduate students act as baby-sitters for "keeping the under-graduates in hand" while "assisting the senior professors in carrying forward their inquiries both within the university or in some private company." The name of the game is to make sure that "money flows out of the government down to the university, where someone hatches a utilitarian idea, and from there [the money flows] over to a company which either makes a product or designs a test." (12:11)

Summary sprinkled with key words and phrases, p. 106.

According to Ridgeway, it is a myth to think the modern university is a "community of scholars" dedicated to teaching and the pursuit of truth for its own sake. Rather "professors are less interested in teaching students than in yanking the levers of their new combines [business interests] so that these machines will grow bigger and go faster." (12:193)

Giving credit: "According to Ridgeway," p. 106-07.

Even if this view of higher education applies only to a handful of big league univer-sities, our college system as a whole must be viewed as a big business. Colleges and univer-sities operate on revenues of $10 billion a year with an annual growth rate of 10 percent. Over two thousand institutions of higher learning employ half a million people and hold about seven million students. (12:2) But this is only part of the story. Nearly all of our primary and secondary schools are geared, in various ways, to mesh with the college system. Overall, Americans spend $58 billion annually on formal education. The only institution that spends more is the Defense Department. Over a fourth of our population-- 60 million youngsters and adults--are con-nected full time with the knowledge industry. (6:F1)

Statistics to support inference that the college system is also a large institution, which amounts to the second premise, p. 14-15, 47, 50-51.

In my view, big education has the muscle
to promote itself while resisting challenges
to reform. The danger is that higher education, like the military, has become a self-
validating, self-perpetuating system with
almost no external checks on its growth and
influence. This seems to be the point of view
of David Hapgood, a senior research fellow at
New York University, who has written:

Ellipsis
marks:
(...),
p. 103-04.

The escalating demand for diplomas in the
marketplace has made education a huge, sluggish
beast, as alert and competitive as a grass-
eating dinosaur... . Blessed with a monopoly
on diplomas and the fastest growth rate in the
nation, the industry is under no pressure to
change. It does not have to hustle its
clients. The product sells itself. (6:F1)

Case study,
p. 51.

Hapgood charges that rampant "diplomaism"
discriminates against thousands of capable,
imminently trainable job applicants, young
and old, who lack degrees or credentials.
Hapgood cites the case of Raymond F. Male
whose appointment as principal of a racially
troubled New Jersey high school was turned down
by a state-level board. Male, who had compiled
an impressive record as mayor of the City of
Princeton, New Jersey, as an administrative
specialist, and as a mediator in conflicts
between the generations, did not possess a
teaching certificate or the required number
of credit hours in school administration.
(6:F1-2) Hapgood comments:

Inference
based on
case study,
p. 52.

In the suburbs [diplomaism] has the effect of
keeping out creative outsiders like Male. In
the cities, the effect is to keep out creative,
but degreeless, ghetto people. (6:F2)

Do degreed or credentialed applicants
make better employees? Not according to a
comprehensive study directed by Ivar Berg of

Columbia University. Berg, a sociologist with
extensive training in business administration
and economics, studied thousands of jobs in all
income levels and concluded that college
graduates did not perform better or produce
more than employees on the same jobs without
degrees. Interestingly, employees with
degrees tended to be more dissatisfied with
their jobs so that turnover among B.A. degree
holders was actually higher than among employees
without degrees. (2:92-94) Berg, a cautious
researcher, comments:

Study,
p. 51.

> The data...do not prove that educational
> requirements are bad; they do, however, rein-
> force doubts about whether the benefits that
> managers apparently believe accompany
> credentials do in fact materialize. (2:101)

Christopher Jenks and David Riesman, two
more sociologists interested in higher education, have summarized a study sponsored by the
American College Testing Program which found
no relationship between grades in college and
later job performance. The study covered the
fields of "business, engineering, medicine,
school teaching, and scientific research."
(9:205) Paul Goodman, a long-time critic of
the schools, insists that "years of schooling
and diplomas" do not predict success in the
less prestigious semiskilled jobs. (5:73)
Berg's study seems to support this contention.
(2:87) Another sociologist, Patricia Sexton,
has written:

Study,
p. 51.

> There is...an absence of evidence that the most
> able in performance of jobs or other real-life
> tasks are selected or produced by the standards
> set and training offered by higher education.
> (13:51)

Ellipsis
marks:
(...),
p. 103-04.

Why then do so many employers insist on
the B.A. degree? According to Sexton,

Note
lead-in to
quotation,
p. 105-06.

"Employers often hire from the degree elite
because of the prestige rather than the superior training or job performance skill attached
to a college degree." (13:51)   Moreover,
employers may prefer applicants with degrees
for certain social reasons.   Sexton cites
several studies to show that college serves
to maintain the social class structure in
America.   Graduates tend to come from the
middle and upper economic ranges of society,
while many capable lower-class youths never
make it to college or drop out in dispro-
portionate numbers. (13:51)   In my opinion,

Writer's
opinion
identified,
p. 107.

the diploma often certifies that the bearer
knows how to dress and talk, comes from a
"good" family, and is white.   The "troublesome"
lower classes have been effectively screened
out, and the men who run the company are
assured of getting eager, obedient young
people most like themselves in origin and
outlook.   Never mind what the graduates learned
in college; they soon will be groomed in the
company's six-week training course for whatever
roles have been assigned to them.

Another study mentioned by Hapgood found
almost no relationship between escalating

Study,
p. 51.

educational requirements and technical changes
in jobs.   John K. Folger and Charles B. Nam
studied a range of jobs that had raised
educational requirements during a ten-year
period.   The researchers found, in Hapgood's
words, that "only 15% of the increased demand
for diplomas could be accounted for by
changes in the nature of work.   The other 85%,
[Folger and Nam] found, was the result of added
diploma requirements for the same job." (6:F2)

These studies show, I think, how wasteful
is the game of diplomaism.   As job qualifications rise, more young people attend colleges,

which in turn must expand their operations. **The problem as applied to colleges, p. 12-13.**
When more graduates apply for jobs, business
again raises its educational requirements--
which sends young people back to school, and on
and on.

How long can the colleges continue such **Deductive conclusion: Colleges are wasteful and self-serving, p. 14-15.**
wasteful expansion before their credibility
suffers, just as the military's has? Perhaps
not too long. The popular press is beginning
to bear omens of a graduate glut. A story by
the Associated Press, for instance, quoted an
official Department of Labor news release which
warned that eight out of ten jobs to be filled
during the seventies will not "require" a
college degree. Associated Press asked, "Is
the present popular attitude that 'everyone **Quoting quoted material, p. 129.**
is entitled to a college education' really
needed?" The story listed the fastest-
growing jobs of the seventies: electronics
technicians, business machine servicemen,
cashiers, hospital attendants, receptionists,
stewardesses, and library technicians--none
requiring the B.A. degree. Associated Press
concluded: "Jobs in the future may require
more schooling than in the past, but that
schooling does not necessarily mean more
college education." [stress added] (10:C1) **Stress added, p. 128.**

Alternatives to College

In my view, gluts of anything have a way **Paragraph of opinion bridging two sections of paper, p. 100-01.**
of making people think twice. Too many
weapons and casualties of war have produced
genuine popular movements to cut back the
military. Too many cars have spurred people
to consider alternative means of transportation.
Too many graduates who may not find the jobs
they think they deserve will, I maintain, move
the nation to scale down its wasteful system
of college education while exploring alterna-

tives to college for learning and job training.

As the popular press reports almost daily, the colleges are now facing a serious financial crisis. (14:III) The dinosaur is floundering. The time seems ripe for a change in our basic outlook on college education.

We might begin by demythologizing college education. Ivan Illich, priest and educational reformer, feels that "the New World Church is the knowledge industry," and it apparently needs a Reformation. Already we have begun to demythologize the military. Thousands of Americans are now questioning what Donovan calls the "sacred trinity of national defense, patriotism, and anti-communism" which sustained the military for years. (3:215) In my opinion, if higher education was regarded not as a national religion but rather as another big corporation with a monopoly on teaching and certification, or a cumbersome bureaucracy that has outgrown much of its original purpose, we might find the boldness to explore alternative ways to learn and prepare for jobs--independent study, correspondence, apprenticeship, on-the-job training, travel, wits, and hard work. Millions of people have found ways to communicate with God and lead spiritual lives without following the program of an organized church; how much can people learn outside college? Indeed, how much have they <u>not</u> learned for all the years they have spent in classrooms?

Illich would also have us consider how helpless and dependent large institutions render their clients. The poor, for instance, have become "hooked" on a system of formal schooling they had no hand in shaping and cannot possibly compete well in, just as they have become "hooked" on distantly regulated

Relating topics (the church, the military, the colleges); general principle: demythologizing institutions, p. 53-54.

Summary, p. 57-58, 103.

welfare programs that destroy their self-respect and their incentive to act on their own behalf. (8:12) But all of us, poor and well off, are hooked on schools. Illich comments:

> School prepares for the alienating institutionalization of life by teaching the need to be taught. Once this lesson is learned, people lose their incentive to grow in independence;...[and] close themselves off to the surprises which life offers when it is not predetermined by institutional definitions... School either keeps men and women for life or makes sure that they will be kept by some institution. (7:24)

Ellipsis marks: (...), p. 103-04. [brackets], p. 104-05.

Illich wants to eliminate what he feels is the wasteful middleman, the school or college with all its buildings, files, business dealings, support personnel, marching bands, and football teams. He believes we should put dollars we normally spend on inefficient formal schooling into the hands of people, young and old, poor and not so poor, so they can seek whatever training they need from free-lancing teachers and working professionals. Illich apparently has faith that people, once liberated from overgrown institutions, can act sensibly on their own behalf and teach themselves what they need to know to become self-sufficient. (7:4)

Summary, p. 57-58, 103.

Paul Goodman wants to get the colleges out of contracted research altogether. He feels that high-level, contracted research has nothing to do with teaching, and has been the single most important cause of the colleges' unwarranted expansion. Let the government and industry conduct their own research, Goodman proposes. The colleges themselves should "drop mandarin requirements of academic

Note lead-ins to quotations, p. 105-06.

diplomas that are irrelevant, and rid
[themselves] of the ridiculous fad of awarding
diplomas for every skill and trade whatever."
In Goodman's view, college teachers should be
working professionals, with or without degrees

Closing
para-
graphs:
possible
solutions
itemized,
p. 8-9,
12-13, 16.

of their own, "who feel duty-bound and attracted
to pass on their tradition to apprentices of a
new generation." Finally, Goodman feels
students should get clear on what they want to
learn and insist they be taught it. But
Goodman, like Illich, also feels much useful
learning can occur beyond the college campus.
He would divert most of the money now spent on
schooling into such projects as local noncom-
mercial TV and radio stations, VISTA and Peace
Corps programs, expanded library services, and
political action groups. (5:75)

Berg would strengthen the nation's
primary and secondary schools rather than
tolerate the continued expansion of higher
education. Berg would also urge society, and
especially employers, to reassess "this
purposeless credential consciousness" which
"handicaps education, especially higher education, in the pursuit of its promise to liberate
people and to help preserve for a society its
better traditions and commitments." (2:190-91)

Ironically, it is the military that,
despite other faults, may point the way toward
a sensible alternative to college for job
training. Berg concludes that the military
has proved to be very efficient in training
young men for skilled jobs, and many of these
jobs have civilian counterparts. According to
Berg, the military has long known that specific
vocational and on-the-job training for military
personnel are better predictors of job success
than years of prior schooling. (2:147, 152)
The military training model, stressing actual

skills and job proficiency rather than grades, degrees, and other irrelevancies, is for Berg a good one for society to adopt for efficiently training people of all ages and backgrounds for jobs. Berg comments:

> The military experience...is substantially subversive of the prevailing ideologies that make so much of marginal increments of formal education. The results [of the study] are interesting, not only because they include data bearing on relatively skilled occupational specialties, but because they are suggestive of the productive potential of a labor market in a nation in which there has been chronic unemployment and, apparently, underemployment of a large number of men and women with allegedly deficient educational credentials. (2:159-60)

Longer quotation, p. 126.

As for myself, I would propose two remedies, one economic, the other legal. I would first channel most funds now spent on the present wasteful college system into creating new institutions of learning along the lines of the proposals of Illich, Goodman, and Berg. Second, I would enact laws to phase out many diploma and credential programs. I agree with Illich that it should be illegal to judge an applicant's worth on the basis of prior schooling. In my opinion, the sole criteria for hiring should be skill, knowledge, and demonstrated potential, and it should not matter where or how the applicant developed these qualities.

Writer's opinions identified, p. 107.

These proposals, I believe, would break the colleges' present monopoly on teaching and job training and allow viable alternatives to flourish. Whoever elected to attend college would do so out of choice, not necessity. The new bare-bones colleges would become true

Conclusion, p. 102.

centers of learning rather than places to
accumulate credits and degrees. The colleges
would have to compete for clients, and the
competition would render them more efficient
and responsive. We Americans generally hold
that competition of this sort is healthy;
why shouldn't it improve our colleges as well?

BIBLIOGRAPHY

1. Beller, Irving. "The Concentration of
   Corporate Power," in Where It's
   At, edited by Steven E. Deutsch and
   John Howard, Harper and Row, 1970,
   p. 92-111.

2. Berg, Ivar. Education and Jobs: The
   Great Training Robbery, Praeger
   Publishers, 1970.

3. Donovan, Colonel James A. Militarism,
   U.S.A., Charles Scribner's Sons,
   1970.

4. Galbraith, John Kenneth. The New
   Industrial State, Houghton Mifflin
   Co., 1967.

5. Goodman, Paul. "Freedom and Learning:
   The Need for Choice," The Saturday
   Review, May 18, 1968, p. 73-75.

6. Hapgood, David. "The Diploma: A Meaningless, if Powerful, Piece of Paper,"
   Los Angeles Times, August 3, 1969,
   sec. F, p. 1-2.

7. Illich, Ivan. "Schooling: The Ritual of
   Progress," The New York Review,
   December 3, 1970, p. 20-26.

8. Illich, Ivan. "Why We Must Abolish
   Schooling," The New York Review,
   July 2, 1970, p. 9-14.

9. Jenks, Christopher and David Riesman.

Bibliography for parenthetical reference system, p. 120-23, 124-26.

The _Academic_ _Revolution,_ Doubleday
& Company, Inc., 1968.

10. "Jobs: Is College Needed?" _The_ _Fresno_
Bee, July 5, 1970, sec. C, p. 1.

11. Mills, C. Wright. "The Structure of
Power in American Society," in
Where _It's_ _At,_ edited by Steven E.
Deutsch and John Howard, Harper and
Row, 1970, p. 83-91.

12. Ridgeway, James. _The_ _Closed_ _Corporation,_
Ballantine Books, 1969.

13. Sexton, Patricia Cayo. _The_ _American_
School, Prentice-Hall, 1967.

14. Trombley, William. "UC Facing Most Basic
Changes in Its History," _Los_ _Angeles_
Times, February 1, 1971, sec. II,
p. 1-2.

AFTERCHAPTER

Activities

1. Compare the two longer papers with the outlines on which the papers were based appearing in Chapter 7. How do the essays deviate from their outlines? Why do you think they deviate?

2. What does the college paper gain or lose by being broader and less well focused than the film paper?

3. What sections of the college paper might have been researched in greater detail? What sections might have been omitted to focus attention on other sections?

4. Enlarge on this statement: "The paper on colleges also represents an attempt to combine several of the strategies for researching a topic and writing about it explained in Chapter 2. The dominant strategy is problem and solution, but the strategies of deduction, cause and effect, comparison, and itemization also appear in the paper."

5. Discuss in class: How did writing your paper add to your knowledge or understanding of your research topic beyond what you learned during reading and note-taking?

6. Discuss in class: In what ways does society need specialists and in what ways does it need generalists?

7. Write a short paper based on any activity above.

11

The Shorter Paper

Like the longer research paper, the shorter research paper is based on reading and note-taking leading to a thesis. The thesis guides the writing of the paper. The paper itself, however, explores a more restricted topic, and it is based on fewer reading sources, usually no more than three, occasionally only one. This chapter discusses several uses for the shorter research papers and how you might write them.

A series of shorter papers

The longer research paper, impressive for its thickness, heft, and apparent commitment, nevertheless has drawbacks. It advances the single, well-wrought point of view when research often yields a number of reasonable points of view, some conflicting, some complementary, some only vaguely related. Even a very long research paper seldom captures everything a student learned or thought or felt while reading and note-taking. A useful alternative to the longer paper for communicating a variety of findings is a series of shorter papers. The series may be based on a single research question or on several different but related research questions. Each paper in the series focuses on a specific aspect of the research topic.

Below is a short paper based on the notes that developed into the longer paper on sound and the art of film, found in the last chapter. The paper explores an interesting aspect of the research topic that was excluded from the longer paper because of the limits imposed by its thesis. The paper also uses a system of textual documentation explained in Chapter 9.

HOW BUSINESS DECISIONS AFFECT THE ART OF FILM

Filmmakers often complain that their creations are constantly being compromised artistically by businessmen who finance films and who are interested only in large returns on their investments. No doubt many worthy films have been damaged artistically by alterations meant to increase box office receipts, but my readings suggest that the development of the art of film has often turned on certain technical innovations introduced by businessmen for strictly commercial reasons. The pattern usually is this: declining attendance spurs businessmen to introduce some gimmick which is overused and crudely exploited; serious filmmakers at first deplore the gimmick, but later on accept it and even use it to advance their art.

The introduction of the optical sound track in 1927 seems to have been the brainchild of studio executives who wanted to attract more people to the movies. In his book, The Liveliest Art, Arthur Knight explains how the first sound films were for the most part "static, photographed stage plays, ... 'all-talking, all-singing' musicals...in which raw sound was exploited in every imaginable way." (p. 148) Naturally, serious filmmakers did not respond agreeably to such excesses of sound, which distracted from the sophisticated visual art they had developed during the silent era.

Later on, however, filmmakers not only accepted sound, but found ways to use it artfully. Ernst Lubitsch, the German director who worked at Paramount Studios, used sound sparingly in his films of the late twenties and thirties, and his audiences, it seems, appreciated rediscovering the possibilities of silence. Alfred Hitchcock showed how sound could be used to connect scenes, and René Clair, a French director, used unexpected sound effects to enhance the action of his films. In his book Film Form, Ivor Montagu, a film critic, has written about the "marriage" of sound and image which finally produced a "higher quality" film "because the range of... ingredients over which the creator or creative groups can exercise control is enormously multiplied." (p. 172)

The advent of wide-screen cinema in the 1950s was also the undertaking of studio businessmen who had to do something to lure the ranks of TV viewers back into movie theatres. The stream of new processes-- Cinerama, Todd A-O, CinemaScope, VistaVision-- generally made money for their backers, but the films produced in wider formats were not distinguished for their artistry. These films exploited the dramatic outdoor setting, the lavish backdrop, and the illusion of depth and speed at the expense of story line and characterization. Scenes were reshot less often to cut expenses and the resulting films were actually less interesting visually than small-screen productions had been once the novelty of the wide screen wore off. Knight comments on the films of this period:

> As shots grew longer and close-ups rarer, it became increasingly difficult for directors to achieve the dislocation of time, the singling out of detail, the freedom of action once implicit in the medium. (p. 298)

Ivor Montagu does not buy the argument of movie executives that wide screen is more "realistic" than the conventionally shaped frame. The issue, Montagu maintains, is not how much the frame should show, but how well the filmmaker can control what audiences see. The filmmaker working in wide-screen format has less control over his medium: "... a screen that depicts an image wider than that on which attention can concentrate will... result in a confusion and amount to anti-art." (p. 292)

The era of ultrawide screens seems to
have passed as the film industry has settled
for a frame size somewhat wider than the pre-
fifties frame but not as wide as the early
exploitative panoramic frame. Knight notes
that by the late fifties directors were
learning to live with the wider frame. Some
directors, such as John Ford and Robert Wise,
have explored new ways "of cutting on movement"
--directing attention to objects in the frame
by the movements of characters. And Knight
suggests that other directors apparently are
discovering that, Montagu's objections aside,
the wide screen offers new possibilities for
composing shots. (p. 300-301) In the future,
according to Knight, filmmakers may shoot films
in frames that can be optically varied in width
and height. The scene, subject, or story line
would determine the shape of the frame.
(p. 305)

    Film is, after all, a mass medium,
financially dependent on a broad patronage.
The businessmen who run the studios must find
ways to keep the industry financially sound.
But the gimmicks they come up with usually
bore moviegoers after a few years. Perhaps
what has really saved cinema in the long run
is the ability of serious directors to transform whatever gimmicks of sight and sound
businessmen force on them into genuine contri-
butions to the art of film.

    Because the text mentions authors, titles of books, and page num-
bers, a bibliography is unnecessary.

The two-source paper: research as "montage"
Let us turn now to strategy. Whether you write a series of papers
on the same research topic, or write different papers on different

topics, you might consider the advantages of looking into at least two different reading sources to research your topic. Information taken from at least two sources often combines in such a way as to produce a unique total effect, much in the same way the film editor joins dissimilar shots to produce a third, greater concept or effect. This advice is not meant to make research superficially arty; it is meant rather to help you learn more about your topic by viewing it from different vantage points.

Here are some suggestions for pairing reading sources to achieve a sort of "montage" of conclusions:

1. *Past and present.* Pair a source describing a contemporary issue with another that provides an historical background for the issue. (Example: Find a magazine article describing the mood of the Catholic Church in the Low Countries, where sentiment for priestly matrimony is very strong. Then read a book about Church history and try to determine just why priests were denied matrimony in the first place. Do the reasons still apply?)

2. *Pro and con.* Base your paper on one reading source that argues in favor of a certain position and another that argues against the position. (Example: Read two sources about financing manned space travel, one calling for increased expenditures, one arguing against spending more money. Which source, in your opinion, presents the stronger case?)

3. *Fact and opinion.* Research a topic by looking into two pertinent sources, one primarily factual or descriptive, one based largely on opinion. (Example: Find a newspaper story that supplies facts about how welfare rolls are increasing. Get a book or magazine article advancing an opinion about how best to get people off welfare. Do the facts of the newspaper story tend to weaken or strengthen the argument of the second source?)

4. *General principle and specific application.* Set a specific issue against a larger backdrop of general principles by which the issue may be better understood. (Example: Find a magazine article or newspaper story describing a certain bill before Congress. Then read a book about the workings of Congress, the activities of lobbyists, and other factors that determine any Congressional bill's chances for passage. What do you think are the chances the bill will be passed or defeated?)

Below is a shorter paper that shows how a general principle might add to an understanding of a specific topic. The general principle deals with a definition of "good" English; the specific topic is American Negro dialect. The paper uses the footnoting system of documentation explained in Chapter 9.

WHAT IS "GOOD" ENGLISH?

One aspect of race relations that whites have not yet begun to confront is language. For while most whites may now be prepared to grant blacks equality in employment, housing, and education, many whites still feel the Negro dialect is inferior and should be replaced with the white "standard" or "correct" English. The study of linguistics, however, suggests that Black English is not inferior, and that objections to it may have a prejudicial base.

The linguist W. Nelsen Francis has noted that "applied to language, the adjective good has two meanings: (1) 'effective, adequate for the purpose to which it is put' and (2) 'acceptable, conforming to approved usage.'" Francis asserts that the second definition is what most people mean by "good" English. People often confuse social acceptability with effectiveness and tend to equate "bad" grammar or pronunciation with questionable character or ability. Francis feels that the first definition of good English should prevail:

> ...the notion that the language of social and educational inferiors is "bad" has been extensively taught in the schools, so that even those who speak it naturally often get the idea that there is something intrinsically wrong without clearly understanding why... . What is called "bad" English in the usual sense may be highly effective in the appropriate context. Conversely, language which is socially and educationally impeccable may be most ineffective, as anyone who has listened to a bad speech can testify.[1]

---

[1] W. Nelsen Francis. The English Language, W. W. Norton and Company, 1965, p. 244-46.

Another linguist, Olivia Mellan, has
described how militant blacks in Washington,
D.C., have objected to the policy of the
schools to "eradicate" Black English because
eradication "brands the speech [the black
student] has used since childhood as defective
and by inference slurs the black culture that
speech expresses."[2]

An alternative to the eradication of
Black English is the eradication of the language
prejudice that many whites still have. The idea
here, as I understand Miss Mellan, is to teach
effective English rather than socially acceptable
English. Presumably, such an approach would
treat all varieties of English as equals so that
a person might be judged on the quality of his
ideas rather than on how he pronounces his words
or forms his verbs. Black English is effective
and adequate for millions of American Negroes
who speak it, just as standard English works
quite as well for many Americans of all colors.
Miss Mellan writes that "linguists who have
studied the vocabulary and syntax of Black
English find it to be a 'separate but equal'-ly
valid language system, with a highly developed
structure of its own." If so, it could be that
Black English might work well even in situations
that normally call for standard English.

But the issue is very complicated.
Language that "doesn't sound right" may indeed
set up certain blocks, however unwarranted, in
the mind of the listener which have the effect
of impairing communication. Perhaps blacks, if
they want to get through, had better use the

---

[2]Olivia Mellan. "Black English," The New
Republic, November 28, 1970, p. 15-17.

white man's brand of English. But this shifts
the obligation to change language habits on
blacks when it is whites who must understand
that a speaker may not "sound right" and still
deserve a fair hearing. Certainly the schools
should educate to produce more effective
speakers, but we need more tolerant listeners,
too, those who don't let color or social class
mask out the voices of people who want to be
heard.

BIBLIOGRAPHY

Francis, W. Nelsen. The English Language, W. W.
    Norton and Company, 1965.

Mellan, Olivia. "Black English," The New
    Republic, November 28, 1970, p. 15-17.

The one-source "jump" paper
  Another type of shorter research paper takes the form of a review
of a single book or article the student found interesting. The paper
may be divided into two parts: first, a summary of those aspects of
the book or article the student found most interesting; second, a
personal comment on what the book or article meant to the student, why he found it interesting or crucial. The student summarizes what he read, then "jumps" to his own opinion based on what
he learned from his reading. Sample "jump paper," informally
documented:

OVERPOPULATION REDEFINED

    The problem of overpopulation usually
leads people to consider such solutions as
family planning, abortion, and contraception.
But an article by Wayne H. Davis appearing in
the January 10, 1970, New Republic made me consider overpopulation in a new way. The title
of Davis' article is "Overpopulated America,"
but the article has almost nothing to say
about limiting the size of families. Davis

is interested not in absolute numbers of people but in the effects of a highly technological society such as ours on the land it depends on.

According to Davis, the crucial factor that determines whether or not a nation is "overpopulated" is its standard of living, how much it consumes, how much it wastes, how much it pollutes the land. Davis compares the United States with India. India has over twice as many people as we do, and yet it would take twenty-five Indians to equal the demands on the land of one American. In "Indian equivalents" the population of the United States is not 200 million but rather four billion. Davis feels that the typical Indian's "contribution to the destruction of the land is minimal"; the average American, on the other hand, will during his lifetime pollute three million gallons of water, demand 21,000 gallons of gasoline, and eat 10,000 pounds of meat. Thus America is the world's most overpopulated country because, as Davis puts it, we are "rapidly decreasing the ability of the land to support human life. With our large population, our affluence, and technological monstrosities, the United States wins first place."

This article has two important implications for me. First, it is obvious that concerned citizens and organizations working to limit the population of the United States will have to attack the problem on a much more fundamental level, one that challenges, perhaps, some of our most cherished beliefs. I myself feel it will be far more difficult to persuade Americans to reduce their standard of living (for that is the heart of the problem) than to convince them they must reform their abortion laws and develop better methods of contraception.

Second, I wonder about the other countries of the world, especially the numerous under-developed countries hoping to achieve a higher standard of living. Does the world have enough resources to allow people of all nations to live as well as Americans? I doubt it. And I don't think the global environment, already threatened, could stand twenty-five times the present level of pollution and ravaging.

The more I learn about ecology and population the more I believe our problems are beyond the reach of technology and government to solve. What we (and I mean the whole world now) will have to do is find a new way of life based on a totally different set of values. I am not sure what these new values should be, but I am certain they cannot be based on unchecked consumption of the earth's raw materials.

The paper of informed opinion

On occasion instructors ask students to write short papers expressing their views on various assigned topics. And while students may have no trouble writing about what they did last summer or why hamsters make good pets, other assigned topics such as disarmament, birth control, or violence may prove more difficult to write about. Students often feel they don't know enough about these deeper subjects to write about them with confidence. But a little research can help, even if an instructor doesn't require it. Papers based largely on personal opinion and experience are usually more effective and enlightened if students take the trouble to read a little about their topics before writing.

Some students feel that it is "cheating" somehow to research topics if instructors expect students to rely mostly on personal opinion when writing. Indeed, it is not cheating to become informed before writing. But what may be construed as "cheating" is a failure to give credit to the writers or sources you use in your paper. You'll want to mention your sources in your paper, although formal documentation may not be necessary. You'll *always* want to use quotation marks if you lift a sentence or two word for word from a source you use in your paper. Similarly, be sure to separate your ideas from those of the writers you rely on, and give credit to the writers for their ideas.

Below is a paper of personal opinion enhanced by research. The paper is informally documented.

DEVELOPING RESPONSIBILITY IN CO-ED DORMS

Should men and women college students be allowed to live together in the same dormitory? Many parents say no. They fear, apparently, that co-ed dorm living would present so many distractions and temptations that their sons and daughters would never find time to study, much less stay out of deep trouble. But going to college is as much a social as an intellectual experience. Co-ed dorm living could provide unique opportunities for young people to mature and accept responsibility, two important reasons for attending college.

College students have no fewer personal problems than any other group of people. Freshmen especially may have trouble adjusting to the rigors of college and a new life away from home. Advanced students may find the competition in their classes very intense, and those with low grades may feel uncertain about their choice of majors. All students, of course, live by tight schedules crowded with long bouts of studying, writing papers, and preparing for exams. Success in college may be determined as much by how well one bears up under these pressures as by one's intellectual capacity.

But friendships established under conditions of mutual loneliness, mental exhaustion, uncertainty, or desperation may not always be healthy or sensible. Rather than relating to each other as human beings who respect each other, students who flee to each other to escape their studies may be more inclined to take rather than to give and to see in the other not a real person but a sex object, a parent figure, a refuge. These relationships may not last, and they may finally do more harm than good.

Many students, of course, do make true friends and enjoy very good relations with each other. But co-ed dorm living could help many other students who have trouble adjusting to college both academically and socially. A recent issue of _Life_ describes a successful experiment in co-ed living at Oberlin College. About 800 students at Oberlin live in eight co-ed dorms with men and women occupying alternate floors. These students eat together, study together, and have unlimited, unregulated visiting hours in each other's rooms. Most Friday nights are spent in what _Life_ calls "identity crisis" sessions where students ask the traditional questions, "Who am I?" and "Where am I going?" Not all students find answers, but no one lacks companionship. The community spirit is apparently strong in Oberlin's co-ed dorms. Students "need" each other, but not in a desperate, physical way. Oberlin psychologist Dr. Martha Verda comments on male-female relationships in the co-ed dorms:

...students don't have to pair off as lovers to get to know each other. They form brother-sister relationships, and take on larger groups of friends.

Life also reports that "an increase in community activity, and a sharing of studies... has not caused grades to drop," and the students who live in these dorms don't seem to have any more sexual problems than any other group of students. Thus parents' fears about co-ed dorms may be unfounded, if Oberlin's experi-

ence is typical. Students of both sexes
living together can regulate their behavior
and learn what it means to be responsible
adults. Grades don't have to suffer under
co-ed living arrangements, and the cooperative,
social nature of learning in these dorms may
be more humane than the highly competitive,
lone-wolf style of scrambling for grades that
students seem now to dislike.

The literary paper

Papers on literary topics can take a variety of forms. They can be long or short. They can deal with a single work of literature or with several related works. They can stress the craft of the writer in constructing a story or shaping a poem. Or they can dwell on the larger thematic implications of the work and how the work provides insights into human nature.

Here is a paper that explores the topic of authority as presented in three short stories written by different authors. The paper is informally documented.

DECENT HUMAN BEINGS MAKE LOUSY AUTHORITIES

The effective authority is one who gives
orders and sees that they are carried out.
Usually these orders are given in the name of
some larger social necessity. But no matter
how urgent or justifiable an order issued by
an authority, the authority can seldom establish truly humane relationships with his
subordinates. Truly humane relationships, I
believe, are based on a mutual perception of
equality and a willingness to regard the other
person as complete and sufficient to himself.
But the authority can never achieve such
rapport with his subordinates. The authority
is the arm of society, manipulating people
for the good of society. Other people to him
are means to the end of sustaining the social
order. I doubt that a person who spends most

of his time manipulating other people can
ever relate fully and humanely to anyone,
whether he has official claims on the other
person or not. If he does attempt to relate
deeply to another person, he must relinquish
his authority, or feel deep guilt.

Such a figure is Sergeant Nathan Marx,
the central character in Phillip Roth's
"Defender of the Faith." Marx is a company
sergeant in an Army training camp. He has just
returned from combat--the story is set in the
closing months of World War II--where he "had
changed enough...not to mind the trembling
of the old people, the crying of the very
young, the uncertainty and fear in the eyes
of the once arrogant." Now he wants to be a
tender person again, to feel and care about
himself and other people. He is a sitting
duck for Private Sheldon Grossbart. Both
Marx and Grossbart are Jews, and Grossbart
exploits his Jewishness to get Marx to grant
him favor after favor. But when Grossbart
pulls strings with another Jew so he won't be
sent to the Pacific, Marx blows up. He is sick
of Grossbart's using people, and he acts
swiftly to get the private shipped out to the
Pacific after all. At first Marx feels his
action is justified: He is "watching out for
all of us," protecting weaker people from the
likes of Grossbart. But at the end of the
story, Marx has second thoughts. He feels
guilty; he has to resist "an impulse to turn
and seek pardon [from Grossbart] for [his]
vindictiveness."

The key to the story is the terse comment, "mercy overrides justice." No matter
how rotten Grossbart, no matter how just the
sentence, Marx realizes that his authority
robbed him of the quality of mercy. To be

merciful would have helped Marx get in touch with himself and others. But society, in this case the Army, can grant no mercy to people like Grossbart, and it falls to authority figures like Marx to carry out society's edict, to defend the "faith" of institutions. This is Marx's fate: to be a tender-hearted authority, a contradiction in terms.

This is also the fate of the unnamed lawyer of the story "Bartleby the Scrivener," by Herman Melville. This story antedates Xerox machines by about a hundred years. Lawyers in those days hired scriveners who copied documents in longhand word for word. Bartleby is a newcomer to the lawyer's office, and while a good copier, he refuses to perform certain other tasks the lawyer asks of him. Bartleby, it turns out, is a strange and moody person who speaks to no one, has an obscure past, and spends a lot of time staring at the wall as if lost in deep philosophical thought. Like Marx, the lawyer is easygoing and at first is willing to grant Bartleby a certain latitude. Soon, however, Bartleby refuses to do any work at all and even goes so far as to take up permanent residence in the lawyer's office. But rather than fire Bartleby outright, the lawyer prefers to move away from him and set up his practice else-where. Bartleby is finally taken to debtors' prison where he dies after refusing to take food.

If Marx felt compassion, so does the lawyer: "I might give alms to his [Bartleby's] body; but his body did not pain him; it was his soul that suffered, and his soul I could not reach." But on a deeper level, perhaps the lawyer feels guilt, as Marx did. A

scrivener's job is dull and dehumanizing; he
is a mere machine, just as later he was replaced
by a machine. Perhaps subconsciously the
lawyer realizes that, in his employer-authority
role, he had related to his workers only as
workers, as means to sustain the economic
order, and not as people. Perhaps too he
senses that he denies Bartleby selfhood in
ordering him to work while Bartleby grows in
selfhood by refusing to work. This awareness
may have motivated the lawyer when, near the
end of the story, he asks Bartleby to come
home with him. Though Bartleby refuses, the
lawyer's offer is still an attempt to relate
to Bartleby as a human being, as an end in
himself, and not as a mere worker.

A different view of authority is supplied
by William Carlos Williams in his story "The
Use of Force." This story is about a doctor
who is called to a house to examine a young
girl who is ill. There has been an epidemic
of diphtheria. But the girl refuses to open
her mouth to admit the doctor's tongue depres-
sor. The doctor is brusque with the embarrassed
parents and finally brutal with the girl. He
forces the examination, explaining that "the
little brat must be protected against her own
idiocy... ." But afterward he realizes that
the possibility of the girl's having diphtheria
was only his excuse for overpowering the girl,
an act bordering on rape, which he admits to
enjoying. Thus the challenge to the doctor's
authority brought out the worst in the doctor,
while Bartleby's challenge brought out the
best in the lawyer.

Marx and the lawyer will probably never
be effective authorities again, but they might
be better human beings. The doctor acts as

we would expect authority to act--decisively,
unwaveringly, in the name of "social necessity"--but in doing so he displays his lack
of humanity and reveals the possibility of
darker motives in those who exercise authority.

AFTERCHAPTER

Activities

1. Compare the short paper on film in this chapter with the longer paper on film in the last chapter. What material occurs in both papers? What new material occurs in the shorter paper? Could the shorter paper have used more material from the longer paper? In what ways (except length) are the two papers similar or different?

2. Reread the longer paper on colleges in the last chapter. How might this paper have been broken up into a series of shorter papers? What thesis sentences for the shorter papers might be derived from the longer paper?

3. For each topic below, supply three related research questions that could lead to short papers. Example:
   Topic: Planned parenthood.
   Questions:
   1. What is planned parenthood?
   2. If planned parenthood doesn't work and the population increases to intolerable levels, what steps, if any, should the government take to curb population?
   3. What groups oppose planned parenthood?
   Topics:
   A. Harvesting food from the sea.
   B. Problems of the working mother.
   C. Automobile safety.
   D. Astrology.
   E. Homosexuality.
   F. The male ego.
   G. A topic of your choice.

4. Match any *three* topics below with appropriate pairs of sources. Briefly explain your choices. Which topics might be explored through more than one pair of sources? Example:
   Topic: Birth control.
   Paired sources: fact and opinion.
   Explanation: First, a source providing facts on the seriousness of the problems of overpopulation; second, a source expressing opinions about how couples might be induced to practice birth control.

Topics	Pairs of Sources
A. Street crime.	1. Past and present.
B. Waste in government.	2. Pro and con.
C. Welfare.	3. Fact and opinion.
D. Mental illness.	4. General principle and specific application.
E. Communes.	
F. Patriotism.	
G. Divorce.	
H. Air pollution.	
I. Race relations.	
J. Mass transit.	
K. Three topics of your choice.	

5. Review Chapter 2. Then analyze each of the short papers in this chapter by tracing the dominant stategy of each. Also trace secondary strategies, if any. (The strategies: itemization, classification, comparison, cause and effect, problem and solution, time, deduction, and relation.) Are any papers not patterned in any of these strategies? If so, what strategies do these papers use for ordering and relating their ideas?

6. Select a topic that interests you. Write three research questions based on the topic. Research each question and write three short papers, each based on a different question.

7. Select a topic that interests you. Pick a pair of source types listed in activity 2 that will help you research the topic. Write a short paper based on your findings.

8. Browse through a book or read a magazine article that interests you. Write a short "jump" paper about the book or article. Conclude your paper with your own reflections.

9. Write a "jump" paper for an assigned essay, chapter, or story.

10. Jot down some notes expressing your views on a certain topic or issue. Read a book or a magazine article about the topic. Write a short paper about the topic and refer to your source to lend authority to your ideas.

12
The Journal

A more informal, sometimes personal approach to research is the keeping of a journal based on readings. The journal takes the place of a longer paper or a series of shorter papers. It combines note-taking, personal reactions, and conclusions which the researcher wants to share with other people.

Unlike diaries, journals are meant to be read by other people. The journal-keeper may be personal, even whimsical, but he should avoid abbreviations and shorthand notation. Journal keeping may or may not lead to the formulation of a single thesis. The researcher may prefer not to point all his findings in one direction. He may instead want to explore several related aspects of his research topic and advance several theses. Or he may want to focus on just one aspect of his topic and advance just one thesis. In any event, research journals usually have this much in common: They begin in a question, a hunch, a desire to know, and end in relative certainty. They represent day-by-day or source-by-source accounts of what was read, why it was read, and what conclusions were drawn. Like notes leading to papers, journals should include summaries, important quotations, and crucial facts and statistics—anything, in fact, that will help the reader understand how the journal-writer drew his conclusions. Some entries may not be based on any reading at all; they may represent conclusions drawn after a period of thinking about earlier entries.

The following journal is based on the same notes that developed into the longer paper about college education, which appears in Chapter 10. The dates of the thirteen entries are fictitious, but the movement of thought is authentic. My purposes are, first, to show how the entries might be spaced over a one-month period, and, second, to invite comparison between two ways of communicating findings about identical research topics.

MARCH 3: I intend to look into the connection between the war in Southeast Asia and our system of college education. My interest in these topics grew from my knowledge that many of our leading universities do research for the military. At present I don't consider this a healthy relationship because the universities risk losing a degree of political and scientific independence if they become too closely allied with the federal government and the military. But I don't want to confine my readings to the war in Southeast Asia; I want to read about large institutions in general.

MARCH 4: I bought a copy of *The Closed Corporation* by James Ridgeway from the Pickwick Book Store and read a few chapters last night. The cover of the book says, "How America's great universities are controlled by big business and the Department of Defense." Ridgeway feels that "the major universities became first captive and then active advocates for the military and para-military agencies of government in order to get more money for research." Ridgeway includes tables in the back of his book showing how much money some of our larger universities get from the Defense Department:

University of Michigan	$21,579,000
Stanford University	20,880,000
Columbia University	31,582,000
University of Illinois	25,064,000
Harvard University	37,328,000
University of California, Berkeley	23,893,000

These figures are for one year, 1966. Ridgeway lists only the "top" 32 universities. I don't know what the total is for all colleges and universities that do defense research, but perhaps I can find out later.

Ridgeway claims that two-thirds of all the money that colleges spend on research comes from the Department of Defense and other war-related agencies. Also, there are many so-called nonprofit research centers connected with universities which get $1.2 billion worth of research contracts every year.

Naturally one wonders if all this money shouldn't be spent on other things.

MARCH 5: I want to add some more notes on Ridgeway's book. Ridgeway feels that professors are "less interested in teaching students than in yanking the levers of their new combines so that these machines will grow bigger and go faster." Perhaps Ridgeway is too harsh on professors, but his point is that all that research money could distract professors from their teaching duties. Ridgeway also maintains that undergraduate students lie in "holding pens" and function mainly to get more money for the university. The more students, the more money from tuition and the more state aid. Graduate students, according to Ridgeway, tell students boring stories, "and students turn to making their own 'free universities' or spend their time hatching political revolutions on the outside."

MARCH 8: A librarian led me to a book by a retired Marine colonel, *Militarism, U.S.A.* The colonel, James A. Donovan, feels the military has grown far too powerful and threatens to dominate our lives. It ties up about $80 billion a year and employs over seven million workers. Donovan feels that there are many groups who have a direct interest in expanding the role of the military. War or no war, the military is bound to go on expanding:

> The Department of Defense has indicated that even if the Vietnam war effort was eliminated, the momentum of various weapons systems already approved or in advance planning, plus existing commitments and other rising costs, would largely consume . . . savings from the decline of hostilities . . . leaving little to provide for the huge and incessant demands of the other pressing domestic problems.

Is all this spending on weapons systems necessary? Donovan feels that the high brass has always oversold us on threats to the nation's security:

> The military has long realized that its existence depends upon the probability or possibility of war and so are rarely optimistic about the intentions or good nature of any potential enemy. The military emphasizes the evil in man and seeks out threats of aggression and danger wherever they may be found.

Donovan quotes *Time,* which asked:

> Who is the enemy, anyway? The Russians, with whom Washington has been signing treaties, and exchanging musicians? The Chinese, who have been shooting Russians lately? Those scrawny North Vietnamese, visited often by American journalists? Assorted revolutionaries in distant and backward countries, who might be influenced by Communists?

I think Donovan (or *Time*) has a point. Are we making all these weapons to meet some phantom enemy?

(But I'm sure the Kremlin has its hawks, too, who think we are going to zonk Moscow tomorrow. There is a danger, I think, in criticizing the military *too* much. We obviously need some kind of defense system; the question is, how much defense is enough, how much is just waste and make-work?)

MARCH 9: Getting back to Vietnam, here are some figures from Donovan's book:

> 40,000 dead.
> 260,000 wounded.
> $104 billion spent.

These figures are for 1969. More waste: $9 billion worth of research projects *canceled* because of various failures. A study by the Defense Department itself revealed that defense contractors with the poorest performance records had the highest profits!

How can we cut back the military? It won't be easy. Donovan feels that the growth of the military is "beyond the control of present democratic processes" to check. All those vested interests.

MARCH 11: I happened to reread a short story I had read some years ago, a story whose theme bears on both the colleges and the military. The story, "The Portable Phonograph" by Walter Van Tilburg Clark, is set in the future after a great war has wiped out most of civilization. The characters in the story are men of great learning and culture who live in crude dugouts in the prairie. It is all they can do to survive in the cold of an approaching winter. As the story opens, three younger men have gathered in the dugout of an old professor who has saved a few books and some recordings of classical music. The professor reads excerpts from great books and plays a recording for his guests on his portable phonograph. The characters seem to worship high culture and the arts, and they are very civil to each other, despite their bleak existence. But at the end of the story, after the others have left, the professor goes to sleep with a "comfortable" piece of lead pipe in his hand. Despite their great learning and civility, the characters really don't trust each other. The professor is overreacting cuddling his lead pipe; the others probably won't rush his dugout and steal his treasures. Even if they do, all of them have missed the point. The irony is that these learned and humane men *should* be able to find a way to live together in peace, but can't.

I'm not sure that professors who conduct research for the Pentagon worship art and high culture. But there is an irony in that the university, which should be a place to seek out truth and teach the truth, is up to its neck in a sort of lie or myth: that we have to build so many weapons to fend off an imaginary enemy. Do these professors really know what they are doing and cynically go about collecting government money, or have they been duped?

MARCH 14: Donovan's book had a lot to say about the Pentagon's dealings with large industrial corporations. (For instance, 2,000 retired military officers sit on the boards of large corporations; they lobby the Pentagon for contracts.) So I thought I'd read something about business. Big business seems to be getting bigger, like the military, and exerts much influence. This is the point of view of John Kenneth Galbraith's *The New Industrial State,* a book that describes a new kind of corporation, one that is allied with the government. A cozy arrangement. The New Industrial Corporation is a slick outfit run by a "technostructure"—a group of specialists who make very few mistakes and who employ scientific methods to induce consumers to buy the corporation's products. The consumer is no longer king; *he* doesn't influence the corporation with his needs and desires. Instead the corporation, through sophisticated advertising, makes him think he has to have this and that. As Galbraith puts it:

> . . . the accommodation of the market behavior of the individual [consumer], as well as of social attitudes in general, to the needs of producers and the goals of the technostructure is an inherent feature of the system. . . . the producing firm reaches forward to control its markets and on beyond to manage the market behavior and shape the social attitudes of those, ostensibly, that it serves.

Only the firm doesn't serve the consumer; the consumer serves it.

MARCH 17: An excursion: I am becoming interested in waste. We waste a lot of money in developing useless weapons systems, and the colleges contribute to the waste. Vietnam was certainly a great waste of men, money, and resources. But how are large corporations wasteful? Galbraith shows how they are very efficient. They have to show a profit; colleges and armies don't. But corporations waste a lot of lives and materials all the same. We have too many cars, too many tape recorders, too many fancy bathtub fixtures, too many useless gadgets. I wonder what fine mind was wasted developing the cassette tape cartridge. I'll admit cassettes are rather handy, but what if that same genius were turned loose on a really worthwhile problem, like desalinating water or designing low-cost prefab homes? What if all the clever engineers could work on solutions to significant problems rather than developing gadgets of marginal value?

I wonder too what would happen if Detroit would let up a little so we could find other ways for getting around. Is the car the only way to travel? Detroit wants us to think it is, and it has been very successful in persuading us the car is the only way to go. Suppose we do have to have cars. Do we need gas-powered cars? Do we need cars twenty feet long? What about those energy cells charged by sunlight that the astronauts use? What's wrong with driving smaller cars for commuting to and from work?

MARCH 22: A friend of mine gave me a clipping from the *Los Angeles Times* about the "diploma racket." David Hapgood, the author, thinks that employers stress diplomas too much. A diploma doesn't mean a man will work better than another man without a diploma. Hapgood cites a study by Ivar Berg who found that workers with diplomas don't produce more or work better than workers on the same job without diplomas. Another study mentioned by Hapgood found that jobs that have increased educational requirements haven't really changed that much. In fact, only about 15 percent of jobs have changed enough (become more technical?) to justify an increase in educational requirements. What does the diploma show? According to Hapgood, "The diploma shows you have conformed enough to be turned loose in adult society."

Hapgood also feels that

> The escalating demand for diplomas in the market place has made of education a huge, sluggish beast, as alert and competitive as a grass-eating dinosaur ... Blessed with a monopoly on the diploma and the fastest growth rate in the nation, the industry is under no pressure to change. It does not have to hustle its clients. The product sells itself.

Education is big business:
1. 60 million people engaged full-time in education.
2. $58 billion spent annually on education.
3. Education's annual growth rate is 10 percent.

Hapgood believes that the diploma has very little to do with learning. It is a way to screen applicants for jobs, a sort of obstacle course which must be run. It assures that not too many people apply for certain positions. But if too many do apply, industry raises educational requirements again, and the colleges get to grow some more. Usually, the increased educational requirements have nothing to do with the actual demands of jobs on employees.

MARCH 23: Waste! Too many applicants for jobs have the effect of raising the educational requirements of jobs; when educational requirements are raised, people go back to school and the colleges expand; as colleges expand they produce more graduates; more graduates produce too many applicants for jobs, so the educational requirements are raised; when educational requirements are raised, people go back to school and the colleges expand; as colleges expand they produce more graduates, more job applicants, etc., etc.

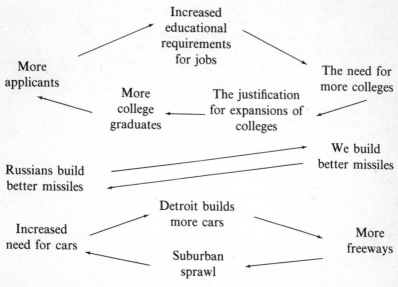

Something is wrong with our institutions.

MARCH 25: My friend Bill is a self-educated painter. He has sold a few paintings now, and an outfit in San Francisco is printing a few of his posters. Bill feels that no one learns to paint in school. Painting must be self-taught. All school can do is provide the opportunity to paint. But society, Bill explains, provides other opportunities to paint, to meet other painters and evaluate each other's work.

Perhaps learning in college is like getting an ulcer. Stress and strain don't always produce ulcers. People have to have a tissue predisposition to develop ulcers. Stress and strain plus tissue predisposition equal ulcers. Teaching doesn't always produce learning. People have to have a mental predisposition to learn. Teaching plus the right mental predisposition equal learning.

MARCH 27: What's wrong with our institutions? I read an article by sociologist C. Wright Mills in which the concept of the "power elite" is advanced. The power elite, according to Mills, is an interlocking triangle of big business, big government, and big military. The power elite makes all the major decisions that affect the nation. The military used to be a relatively minor and isolated institution, but now it dominates government and business, and dominating government and business it dominates us all. Mills' power elite seems to be another term for the military-industrial complex.

Mills doesn't feel the colleges are a member of the power elite, but I do. The colleges, in their own way, have grown just as powerful and wasteful as the military.

MARCH 30: Ivan Illich is a priest and social reformer who has written:

> The escalation of the schools is as destructive as the escalation of weapons but less visibly so.

Illich feels that schools teach the need to be taught. They rob people of their inclination to teach themselves. They also make people dependent on other institutions. Schools certify learning; the existence of schools, and people's dependence on them, implies that learning that takes place out of school is untrustworthy, illegitimate. Schools teach people that to learn is to be taught—in school. Learning out of school is not considered true learning.

Illich makes some interesting comparisons between the school and the church. He feels that education is the "New World Church." Just as the church divides the world into two realms, the holy and the profane, the schools divide the world into two classes, those certified and those who are uncertified. The excommunicant is doomed, banished forever from heaven. The dropout is forever denied the joys of middle-class buying, acquiring, consuming.

Maybe the colleges need a Reformation, a breaking up into many smaller competing "denominations" or alternatives.

APRIL 2: In my view, the effect of the tragic war in Vietnam has been to reveal the wasteful, unchecked growth of the military and of those universities that contributed to the war. But beyond this, if the goals of a large military can be questioned, why not those of other institutions? Why not question Detroit? Why not question our overgrown system of college education?

The problem, as I see it, is this: Some of our institutions, college included, have lost sight of their original goals. They have grown so large and have been so successful in promoting themselves (and have made certain cozy arrangements with other large institutions) that they no longer serve their clients. The clients *think* they are being served, but they are not. These institutions need to be scaled down to manageable size, and new, smaller, more responsive institutions need to be given the chance to develop so that people have a real choice. But we need to watch these new institutions as well: before we know it, they will get out of hand too.

AFTERCHAPTER

Activities

1. Compare the journal in this chapter with the longer paper on college education in Chapter Ten.
   A. Which format is easier to follow? Why?
   B. Which seems better organized? Why?
   C. What material is presented in the paper but not in the journal? What material appears in the journal but not in the paper? Might the journal have been improved by using more material from the paper? Might the journal have been improved by using less material from the paper? What is meant by "improved"?
   D. What are some other similarities or differences between the two approaches?

2. The journal of this chapter states no specific research question, but which entry or entries imply a question? Write out the question. Do later entries imply additional, related questions? If so, write these out too.

3. Does the journal finally pose a thesis? If so, which entry or entries contain it? Might there be more than one thesis implied? Write out (or copy) the main thesis and all related theses.

4. Select a topic to research. Formulate either one research question about the topic or two or three related questions. Now locate at least four sources pertaining to your question or questions. Read and keep a journal based on your readings. Plan at least eight entries for your journal. Try to pose a thesis in the one or two concluding entries.

5. If your findings for the journal you kept for activity 5 seem too scattered or inconclusive, write a paper based on your strongest entries. Complete additional reading and note taking if you have to. Write the paper to sharpen the focus of your thesis and organize material related to the thesis.

13
The Discussion Group

In one sense, independent study is never altogether independent, nor should it be. The student who studies on his own often depends on teachers, librarians, bookstore clerks, and occasionally on other students. This chapter is about dependent study—team study, really. The team doesn't produce a paper; instead it has a discussion. It produces an exchange of ideas. The members of the group stimulate each other and bring out each other's best ideas. The discussion is a sort of "happening," but unlike a noon-hour rally or a rock concert, this happening has direction and purpose. It doesn't merely go on and on and suddenly end. It fills out its alloted time with ideas that mature. Its members may not always agree, but they should break off their discussion with clearer ideas than what they started with, and they should have some respect for each other's ideas.

Discussion groups can take up any topic or question of interest to all the members of the group, but traditionally discussion groups are problem oriented. The members of the group research a number of aspects of a problem and its solution, and then meet to compare notes and come to conclusions. The spirit of discussion is highly cooperative. The goal is to pool knowledge for a common cause. Vigorous debate often finds its way into group discussion, but no single member should seek to "win" simply for the sake of winning. Debate in group discussion should be constructive and meant to help the members of the group understand issues and reach conclusions.

Some typical problem-oriented research questions for discussion groups to research:

1. What is the difference between drug use and drug abuse?
2. What alternatives to the automobile might feasibly be developed?
3. How might the divorce rate among teenagers be reduced?

4. How should our prison system be reformed?

5. What can Detroit do to build safer automobiles?

Often members of discussion groups elect to pursue individual questions all related to a more general group question. Example:

Group question: How should our prison system be reformed?

Individual questions:

1. What special problems apply to youthful offenders?
2. What problems apply to hardened criminals?
3. How can parolees be prepared to reenter society as responsible citizens?
4. What is the relationship between punishment and rehabilitation?

These questions are not mutually exclusive—on purpose. While each researcher has his own focus, each too will likely research material of interest to the other members of the group. Information that one researcher overlooked or couldn't find may have been uncovered by another researcher. The purpose of the discussion is to share information in such a way as to create a sort of complete picture, with each member contributing his fair share and helping out the other members whenever he can.

Below is an edited transcript of a fairly successful group discussion about the problem of overpopulation. The members of the group exchanged ideas before an audience—fellow students in a class—which stood to benefit from the discussion as much as the members of the group. The group used a moderator—one member of the group who helped coordinate research and who made sure the discussion moved along toward conclusions.

TRANSCRIPT: A RESEARCH TEAM DISCUSSES OVERPOPULATION

MODERATOR: We chose to research the topic of overpopulation. We decided to focus on the problems facing underdeveloped countries in reducing or controlling their populations. Specifically, we wanted to know what steps could feasibly be taken on a short-term basis to control population. All of us looked into a variety of solutions, but each of us also agreed to concentrate on one aspect of this problem. Andy consented to collect background information on the subject of world population. Barbara decided to look into educational solutions. Carla agreed to research the area of birth control —abortion and contraception; and Dexter researched some technical and scientific aspects of the problem.

Perhaps we should first establish that overpopulation is in fact a very real problem. Andy, could you give us some idea of the scope of the problem?

ANDY: Basically, it's a numbers game—too many people, too little food. There are almost four billion people in the world today. In about thirty-five years the world's population will double. It will double again in about half that time. The doubling time gets shorter and the population grows geometrically.

MODERATOR: But it can't go on doubling indefinitely because people will starve to death first, isn't that right?

ANDY: That was the theory of Thomas Malthus, an English scientist who lived about two hundred years ago. Malthus believed that mass starvation was inevitable because population increases geometrically while the food supply, if it increases at all, increases only arithmetically.

BARBARA: Which means population doubles much faster than the food doubles.

CARLA: Another aspect of the problem is how the birth rate is highest in the world's poorest countries, the countries that can't afford more roads, schools, hospitals, and so on. The birth rate is about 20 births per 1,000 people in advanced countries and about 45 births per 1,000 in underdeveloped countries.

ANDY: And another way to put the problem is this: The population of advanced countries will double in seventy or eighty years while the population of poorer countries will double often in only twenty years. Unless wars or other catastrophes reduce the population, millions of people will starve to death.

DEXTER: But I want to ask Andy: Isn't Malthus's theory rather out of date now? Isn't it possible to increase the world's food supply in ways that Malthus never dreamed of?

ANDY: Enough to keep up with the population explosion?

DEXTER: Well, I read how it is possible to grow food now in desert places by irrigation. In California, for instance, they pipe in water from several hundred miles away. We have the know-how to get water to arid regions.

ANDY: What about mountainous or rocky regions?

DEXTER: Well, of course, that's a different story.

CARLA: Paul Erhlich, the ecologist, agrees that we have the technology to make deserts bloom, but he points out that few countries have the money or the political tools to undertake vast irrigation or desalination projects. (To Dexter:) You mentioned California. Not many underdeveloped countries can afford water projects as costly as California's.

MODERATOR: Isn't all this sort of beside the point? Most of the hungry people in Asia, Africa, in Latin America don't live in deserts anyway.

DEXTER: Good point. But I have some other information I'd like to share with you. Let me suggest what technology is now capable of doing, or is nearly capable of doing. Scientists have already developed low-cost fertilizers capable of increasing yields by 50 percent. And when these fertilizers are combined with certain chemicals, the yield of crops can be doubled. Recently an American agronomist—a sort of crop specialist—developed a strain of wheat that is extremely high in protein. The object, I think, is to produce not only more food, but food that is higher in energy value.

MODERATOR: I read where agronomists are also trying to develop crops that can be eaten whole—if you know what I mean.

DEXTER: Oh, yes. Thanks for reminding me. Usually, you know, people eat only the seed of a plant, such as wheat, or the stalk, such as celery, or the roots, such as carrots. Now agronomists are developing varieties of edible plants which, as you say, can be eaten whole—seeds, flowers, leaves, stalk, roots, and bulb. And then there is the sea as a potential source of food. Some scientists feel that sea algae can be cultivated in large quantities. Two-thirds of the earth's surface is ocean, you know. We may not ever run out of algae for food. The trouble is, harvesting the sea is at present much more costly than cultivating land. And algae make a rather nasty tasting dish.

MODERATOR: Well, if people are hungry, they will eat anything, I guess. But what about our original question about short-term remedies?

DEXTER: Nothing I've mentioned is really too far beyond the reach of science. In fact, I tried to read about technological programs that could be put into effect relatively soon. I really feel the answer lies with science and technology.

BARBARA: Well, I'd like to argue that point. Perhaps not argue, but take a new tack. It seems to me we should be discussing how to reduce the world's population so we don't have to grow so much food. I think I agree with Malthus. Some day the world will wake up to the fact it has far too many mouths to feed. If the world is to avoid the big die-off that Malthus predicted, we should work on reducing the population somehow. I don't think technology can do enough in the long run to find ways to feed everyone.

ANDY: Yes, but is it possible to reduce the world's population on a short-term basis? We can't just shoot people. The millions of women of childbearing age alive now will go on having children for some time—decades.

BARBARA: Yes, I know. And it really worries me. Dexter here is optimistic, but I'm not. I think the world is in trouble in two ways. First, it isn't really possible to significantly reduce or control the world's population in the next generation. As you point out, there are just too many women of childbearing age. Second, unlike Dexter, I don't feel we can eventually produce enough food. I foresee a massive die-off.

ANDY: Every second someone in the world dies of starvation. Tic, tic, tic—three deaths.

MODERATOR: (to Barbara:) But now what about your research area —education. Can't these women be taught to practice birth control?

BARBARA: That's why I'm so gloomy. No. I really don't feel education is the answer. Not in the short run. In India, for instance, the government has for some time conducted a vigorous, nationwide family planning program. Before the program began India's population was increasing at the rate of 1.3 percent a year with a total population of 370 million. Sixteen years later—sixteen years of education for family planning—the rate had jumped to 3 percent and the population was over 500 million. Too often birth control programs run into all sorts of resistance. People associate having a lot of children with masculinity, fertility, and so forth. Catholics, of course, are forbidden to have abortions. They feel that abortion is murder since the embryo has a soul and is therefore a human being.

DEXTER: Do you buy that argument?

BARBARA: Well, I'm not Catholic, but I do feel abortion cheapens life. I happen to believe any form of life, no matter how primitive or immature, is precious. But that's just me.

MODERATOR: Well, then, what about contraception? Is there any hope of educating women to practice contraception?

BARBARA: The pill, of course, has to be taken regularly. I understand they have had great success in teaching women in Puerto Rico how to use the pill. But in India a program to induce men to have vasectomies has not been too successful. Again, most men in these countries associate the ability to impregnate with manliness, and that's very understandable, I think. If we are talking about short-term solutions, I think we must recognize that educational programs, to be effective, must somehow alter the traditional values and outlooks of a people—almost a contradiction.

MODERATOR: What do you mean?

BARBARA: Well, no short-term, quickie, crash educational program is likely to change the thinking of a people who have practiced certain habits or held certain views for centuries. It's impossible. And even if a people's habits and views could be changed overnight, should they be? I mean wouldn't this cause serious social problems, confuse people and so on? People have a right to maintain ties with their past.

MODERATOR: Let's take stock now. Perhaps we should note that the problem of the overpopulation of poorer countries is as much a technical as a cultural problem. Barbara is pointing out that any all-out effort to reduce overpopulation is bound to disrupt cultures to some extent. The various scientists and technicians have to recognize that.

DEXTER: Personally, I feel the world can't afford to be sentimental about tradition in the face of starvation.

BARBARA: (good naturedly) There's your scientist for you!

DEXTER: (to Barbara:) But I see your point. And I say it is all the more reason to concentrate on increasing the food supply rather than reducing the population. I suspect there is less resistance to growing more and better food than to having fewer babies.

MODERATOR: Possibly. Now let's hear from Carla, who looked into contraception and abortion. Carla, what did you learn that might help us?

CARLA: I gathered a lot of information about the better-known contraceptives. The pill seems to be very effective. Only 1 percent of women who take it correctly will become pregnant.

DEXTER: What about these harmful side effects we have been hearing about?

CARLA: It's true that some women gain weight, get headaches, or feel depression while taking the pill. Others have trouble with blood clotting, and a few women will get cancer of the breast and cervix. The pill is not 100 percent safe, but according to a Dr. Robert Kistner of Harvard Medical School, the dangers of the pill may have been exaggerated. Dr. Kistner feels the pill is safer than becoming pregnant. In other words, a woman runs higher risks when she becomes pregnant than she does if she takes the pill.

MODERATOR: (to Carla:) But what about this problem of education that Barbara sketched for us?

CARLA: I agree that it will be very difficult to induce women in poorer countries to begin taking the pill, and even harder to teach them to take it regularly. The pill, you know, actually increases fertility. Women who skip taking it for a few days may be even more susceptible to becoming pregnant than women who don't take it, and if they do become pregnant they stand a higher chance of having twins. So the pill can backfire.

But I also read about new research in contraception. Research doctors are trying to develop a pill which only has to be taken once a month. Another approach is to implant a tiny capsule in the female which will make her infertile for as long as it is in. And then there has been research into a male contraceptive pill. The object of all of these efforts is to find the perfect contraceptive device—foolproof and easy to use.

BARBARA: (to no one in particular) We need a good pill for men. Why should women have to fool with pills and devices all the time?

CARLA: Let me say a few words about abortion. In Japan, the government has made abortion available to anyone, young or old, married or single, at low cost. The government has also promoted family planning, and it seems to have been successful. Japan's population is leveling off.

BARBARA: Yes, but don't forget Japan is an advanced country. Its people are better educated than India's. The question is, will massive public information programs work in underdeveloped countries where people are perhaps less willing to change?

ANDY: (to Barbara:) But I read where recently the Japanese government has sort of deemphasized its family planning program because it feels it should have a lot of people for cheap labor. A scarcity of workers, you know, drives wages up.

MODERATOR: Then here is another aspect of the problem: economic and political. A lot of countries on the verge of industrialization may not want to control their populations because they feel they need the manpower for their expanding economies.

ANDY: But that works two ways. A condition of too many people may have adverse political and economic effects. Aldous Huxley says that many wars are caused by overcrowding and famine. The emerging nation that wants to maintain a high birth rate for economic reasons may find itself with a revolution on its hands.

BARBARA: My head is starting to hurt. The whole thing is very complex. There don't seem to be any easy solutions.

MODERATOR: Well, at any rate, we should come to some conclusions, and I think we have. Would you agree that the problem of overpopulation has these dimensions I've jotted down here: technical and scientific, medical, educational, cultural, and also economic and political?

ANDY: Maybe we should have concentrated on just one or two.

DEXTER: But then we wouldn't have gotten the total picture.

MODERATOR: Now which of these aspects of the problem might be attacked or worked on in the near future?

BARBARA: I suppose I have to agree with Dexter that in the short run we should work on increasing the food supply. Science and technology must be employed.

ANDY: But Carla has shown how medical science may be on the verge of developing better contraceptive devices.

BARBARA: Still, there's the problem of inducing people to use these new devices.

CARLA: (to Barbara:) You know more about the educational aspects of the problem than I do, but I feel that as contraception is improved—made simpler—the educational barriers will not be as great.

MODERATOR: Perhaps ideally the solution involves both more food and better contraception. The world needs a contraceptive that is easy to learn to use and somehow doesn't clash with local customs and beliefs.

I don't wish to end this book on a note of gloom and doom. Perhaps Barbara's skepticism is justified, but if people could work together as well as this group did, perhaps we can avert apocalypse. This book has stressed the lone researcher teaching himself what he feels he needs to know, and I think there is great dignity in self-sufficiency of this sort. But in the long run perhaps it is better to pool knowledge than to hoard it. The lesson of the discussion group is that our independently drawn conclusions are perhaps more useful when shared with other people whose findings might interest us.

Activities

1. What do you feel is the difference between a group discussion and a bull session?

2. What is the purpose of having a moderator for a group discussion? How might a discussion group get along without a moderator?

3. Explain how the moderator attempted to cut short fruitless digressions and point the group toward conclusions. How successful was he?

4. On what issues did the group finally agree? On what issues did they not agree?

5. Reread the transcript of the discussion and cite examples of how members assisted each other in drawing conclusions by pooling their findings.

6. React to this exchange:
   ANDY: Maybe we should have concentrated on just one or two [aspects of the problem.]
   DEXTER: But then we wouldn't have gotten the total picture.

7. Reread the problem-oriented research questions that appear on page 188. For each question, pose at least three specific questions for individual researchers. Consult the examples on page 189.

8. Team up with two or three other students interested in the same problem and research possible solutions. Discuss your findings before your class. You might consider this schedule:
   First meeting: Get clear on the problem. Decide whether or not you wish to elect a moderator who will serve also as research coordinator. Decide now on individual research questions. Plan a second meeting about midway during the period you have alloted for research.
   Second meeting: During this meeting, discuss preliminary findings. Share working bibliographies. The coordinator should tactfully query each member of the team to determine if special problems have arisen. He should also make sure the team is more or less together on the nature of the problem and the general line of inquiry the group should take. The coordinator may also want to ask the group if it wishes to pose new questions based on first findings. An optional third meeting might be scheduled a day or so before the discussion takes place.
   Third meeting: (optional) The purpose of this meeting is not so much to "rehearse" the discussion as to gain some agreement about the general direction the discussion should take.

9. After your discussion, write a paper based on your individual findings and what you learned from other members of the group during the discussion.

INDEX